Flash Writing

*How to Write, Revise and Publish
Stories Less Than 1000 Words
Long*

Michael Wilson

"Flash Writing: How to Write, Revise and Publish Stories Less Than 1000 Words Long," by Michael Wilson. ISBN 1-58939-637-5.

Library of Congress Control Number: 2004113383

Manufactured in the United States of America.

To Kristen, for all of your support
and love over the years

Acknowledgments

There are many people involved in a project of this size and I have many to thank.

Julie Campitelli, Rachelle Gorland, Shannon Jackson-Arnold, Guillermo James, Gina Johnson, Lynn McLish, CJ Pryor, Phil Raynes, Nita Sweeney, and Amy Warren all for their critiques and revision suggestions. Melissa Hess for the cover design of the book. Lori Ruediger for her extraordinary editing at a pittance of what her editing talent is truly worth.

I want to thank all of the story contributors for agreeing to take a chance on stranger who contacted them via e-mail about their story. I want to thank Debi Orton of *flashquake* (www.flashquake.org), and Mark Budman and Sue O'Neill from the *Vestal Review* (www.vestalreview.net) for hooking me up with the authors of the stories and giving me the editor's viewpoint about flash fiction. I also must thank all of my students over the last eight years who have encouraged and pushed me to write this book.

I especially thank Matt Young for being such a good friend and being supportive of my writing endeavors.

Most of all thanks to my wife Kristen and kids Leah, Benjamin and Isaac, for tolerating all of the hours spent in the workshop working on the book. I love you all with all of my heart.

Introduction

I'm the kind of guy who reads introductions. I always want to hear a little from the writer who created the book. I want to touch the magic that writing is about. I want to know the struggles the writer had. I want to know what he ate for breakfast when he wrote. I want to know what books inspired him. I want to know what he keeps on his desk for inspiration. What I do know now is that there is no magic in writing at all, just work. It doesn't matter what you eat, read, what is on your desk, or on your mind. Writing takes time away from TV, family, eating out with friends, and envelops any leisure time you have left. You write, polish, rewrite, edit and rewrite again. You write until you are sick of the project and feel as if you can't write another word, and then you do it again.

To tell you the truth, I'm not quite sure how I got started with flash fiction. Maybe the seed was planted when I read an article on the Web. Maybe when I was in the library one day and on a whim picked up *Flash Fiction: 72 Very Short Stories*, edited by James Thomas, Denise Thomas, and Tom Hazuka. I'm really not certain. But I needed to shape the content for a day-long class, and somehow flash fiction struck me as a good strategy. What I do know with certainty is that flash fiction has become one of my most popular classes. In 2004 alone, I've been asked to do presentations on flash fiction at the Maumee Valley Writers Conference, the Columbus Writers Conference, and the Thurber House. I've taught one flash fiction workshop and have delivered flash fiction presentations for two other writers' groups.

Flash fiction meets a need in today's reading audience. Sue O'Neill of *The Vestal Review* thinks that it is popular "in part because we're an ADD society-we want a lot in a small space and time. We want instant sizzle." And let's face it, writers have a lot of competition out there for the scarce leisure time available to our audience — hundreds of cable TV channels, millions of Websites, thousands of new books published each month, more time spent working just to keep one step ahead of the creditors. But if we don't have time to read a novel or a lengthy magazine article, we can find five minutes to read one good story. In fact, we can read two or three, or even more, flash fiction stories at the end of the day when we're too tired to concentrate on anything meatier. As writers, we can have the great satisfaction of creating a complete flash fiction story in 15 to 30 minutes a day, where novels and other fiction demand much, much more time.

So when I began teaching flash fiction and looked for books specifically about writing it, I didn't find any. I found a lot of articles and advice online about writing flash fiction, and as a topic in a few fiction writing books, but no books devoted solely to writing flash fiction. A light went on! I would write a book on this subject — a book that would help you get started writing your own flash fiction, teach you about what sets it apart from other fiction, and also cover elements of good fiction writing in general. I would pack the book with good writing exercises to help you learn and hone flash fiction techniques, and I would provide a few story examples to guide you along.

And now the book is finished. I hope you enjoy it and that it stimulates your creativity.

Michael L. Wilson
Lancaster, Ohio
September 30, 2004

Table of Contents

Chapter 1

What is Flash Fiction?

Flash fiction is exactly what it sounds like — fiction that can be read in a flash. But here are some other names, according to Pamelyn Casto's article *Flashes on the Meridian: Dazzled by Flash Fiction*:

> *Other names for it include short-short stories, sudden, postcard, minute, furious, fast, quick, skinny, and micro fiction. ... In China this type of writing has several interesting names: little short story, pocketsize story, minute-long story, palm-sized story, and my personal favorite, the smoke-long story (just long enough to read while smoking a cigarette).*

Flash fiction has been here for centuries under a variety of aliases: myths, fables, parables, fairy tales, nursery rhymes, tall tales, and legends. It also appears in the modern age under names such as: ghost stories, urban legends, rumors, and jokes.

The length of flash fiction is between 250 and 2,500 words, but most publications set the limit at 1,000.

Despite their brevity, these stories are complete stories. They have a definite beginning, middle, and end. They have character, conflict, and all of the other elements that define a short story, except that they are intensely compressed.

Resurging popularity

Flash fiction is well-suited for 21st century readers. With hectic schedules, long hours at the office, and shuffling the kids to soccer practice, there is a demand for stories that can be read quickly and yet still satisfy the reader.

The Internet has also changed the way we read, by stressing short, engaging writing that gets right to the point, without requiring us to scroll down the page to read it.

Online e-zines and literary journals love sponsoring contests for the best flash fiction. It is a wonderful, low-risk method for finding new writing talent. Even mainstream publications such as *Esquire*, *The New Yorker*, and *Vanity Fair* publish flash fiction.

Whatever you call it, flash fiction is here to stay.

Flash Fiction is Good for Writers

Many best-selling authors such as David Foster Wallace, Joyce Carol Oates, Margaret Atwood, and John Updike have recently produced fiction in this format. But writers have always embraced the short-short story form. Writers like Ernest Hemingway, Raymond Carver, and Anton Chekhov have all written flash fiction.

So why should you write flash fiction?

Low risk, little time investment

If you spend two years of your life writing the Great American Novel that sucks, well, you wasted two years of your life.

Flash fiction is low-risk. If you write a terrible flash fiction story, you might have invested a few hours in it. You can move on to the next story and try again.

It does not involve as much of a commitment as writing a lengthy short story or a novel does. It provides instant gratification. In less than a day, you can have a completed (and possibly publishable) story to show for your efforts.

Great way to improve your writing skills

Writing flash fiction makes you aware of every word you choose. You learn to write well using as few words as possible. In flash fiction, you need to know the elements of good fiction and how they work together.

It is far easier to write a long story, wasting words, wandering off on tangents, introducing interesting characters that have nothing to do with the main story. But flash fiction is coiled like a spring. There is no wasted energy in flash fiction. Every word in your story counts and drives you toward the conclusion.

It is fun!

You probably won't get rich writing flash fiction, but you may gain some recognition and respect from well-written stories. But most of all, writing flash fiction is fun. My students are always amazed at what they produce during a flash fiction writing session. They can't believe that their imaginations can create such beautiful works in such a short time.

Elements of Powerful Flash Fiction

Flash fiction contains most of the following elements in every single story:

- **Brevity** — Flash fiction tells a complete story in 1,000 words or fewer.

- **Character** — All fiction requires characters, or at least some sort of presence through which the story is told. The reader identifies with the characters in the story.

- **Surprise Endings** — Flash fiction is famous for its twist endings which often shock the reader.

- **Rich Language** — Flash fiction exists somewhere between the realms of poetry and short story and uses poetic language to weave the tale efficiently.

- **Action** — Even though flash fiction doesn't have a lot of words, a lot of action is packed into each story. Something has to happen during the course of the story.

Do It!

These activities support the concepts of this chapter.

1. Read all of the story examples in Appendix A. (If you don't, I'll be ruining the surprise for you because I use them to illustrate points throughout the book.)

2. Borrow or buy one of the story collections listed in Appendix B, Suggested Reading.

Writing Exercises

Use these exercises to practice your timed writing skills. Write for 10 minutes about each of the following topics:

1.   A man-made disaster

2.   A sinister thing hidden in your closet

3.   A mythical creature living in the modern world

4.   A letter you receive from someone after he/she dies

5.   A buried treasure

First Lines

1.   Where did your mother go?

2.   What am I supposed to do about it now?

3.   How long have you been spying on us?

4.   He was the geekiest boy in the entire 8th grade...

5.   At that moment she knew that something was terribly wrong...

Quick Topics

- Brown bag
- Bucket
- Shack
- Big idea
- Legs

- Dry cleaner
- Raid
- Oh boy
- Carbon monoxide
- Festival

Chapter 2

The Flash Fiction Writing Process

The flash fiction writing process goes through the same steps that all other writing projects do. The stages of the writing process are:

- Idea Gathering
- First Draft
- Shaping
- Second Draft
- Polishing
- Publishing

Each stage requires different skills and strategies. Many writers try to write one perfect story at the very beginning of this process, quickly find themselves frustrated or blocked, and stop writing altogether. Each phase of the writing process calls for specific combinations of skills that should be applied in the right sequence to be most effective. For example, if you try to edit your work before you've even completed a first draft, the results can be dreadful.

Let's review the stages of the writing process and the skills needed for each.

Idea Gathering

Skills required: Discipline; strong desire to write; research techniques; creativity; observation; awareness.

The idea gathering stage is where you open the floodgates of your mind and allow everything to rush out. You allow yourself to believe that anything is a good topic for writing.

Your objective is to generate as many ideas as possible and tap into your imagination for originality. Once you have generated these ideas, store them for later use.

First Draft

Skills required: Discipline; speed; ability to turn off the critical mind; passion; bravery; honesty.

This is where you are often tempted to re-write sentences, change word choices, and otherwise water down your words. The conflict between your natural creativity and your Inner Critic is at its peak.

The goal of this stage is simple: Get the draft down. Get the words on paper before you even think about fixing them up. Do not rewrite. Do not pause for inspiration. Do not think too much about your words. Just write.

Shaping

Skills required: Objectivity; knowledge of the flash fiction form; intuition.

Here you begin reviewing what you have written with an open mind, not necessarily to polish it and correct all of the technical errors that you have made, but to review it with compassion and sensitivity. What is working about this piece? What don't you like? What feels fake? What seems totally believable?

Is it a story? Does it have an ending? Does it have interesting characters? What happens in the story? What is it missing?

Shaping may involve further flash writing drafts to create additional information or detail for your stories.

Second Draft

Skills required: Objectivity; ability to elicit and process feedback from others; eye for detail.

Use what you have learned from writing the first draft and shaping stages to rewrite your story, making changes as you identify them. This is where you could share your work with others to get feedback and improve it.

Polishing

Skills required: Knowledge of (or the ability to look up) grammar, parts of speech, usage, spelling, punctuation, and other polishing tools; detachment; ability to apply knowledge of the flash fiction form to revise the story.

As a flash fiction writer, you will spend a lot of time in the polishing stage. This is where you make the difficult choices about your work. You must hack words and ideas from the story mercilessly if they do not work within the flash fiction form. You release your Inner Critic to correct those grammar, spelling, and usage mistakes that are present within your work, and apply your knowledge of the flash fiction format to polish the story with gleaming insight and energy.

Publishing

Skills required: Market knowledge; sales ability; ability to follow instructions precisely; electronic and paper manuscript formatting.

Publication is not as hard as many people would have you believe. Writers who make intelligent decisions about their work follow the writer's guidelines that every publisher makes available to them. They must be read and followed. If you know your market and follow instructions, you are already ahead of 90% of the other writers out there.

Summary

In upcoming chapters, this book will cover these stages in greater detail, as well as give you specific advice on how to apply this knowledge for writing flash fiction.

Do It!

These activities support the concepts of this chapter.

1.   Go online and check out websites about mythology, ghost stories or urban legends, and spend time reading the ones that interest you.

2.   Go online and read stories from the flash fiction sites listed in the Online Resources section in the back of this book.

Writing Exercises

Use these exercises to practice your timed writing skills. Write for 10 minutes about each of the following topics:

1. A hot day

2. An unusual day at the mall

3. An ice cream truck accident

4. A high school reunion

5. Someone who can no longer fit into his/her clothes

First Lines

1. There were worse things that could have happened, but I couldn't think of any at this time...

2. He lost it. I could tell by the look in his eyes...

3. Where are you going with that thing?

4. She brought the dog home and hid it in the garage...

5. You are crazy if you think that you're going to get away with this...

Quick Topics

- Peanut butter
- Taco
- Barefoot
- Flattering
- Spam

- Renaissance
- Vertigo
- Pump up
- Serendipity
- Bad advice

Chapter 3

Preparing to Write Flash Fiction

To write flash fiction you need to immerse yourself into the flash writing mindset. Doing this requires you to do two things:

First, you need to familiarize yourself with the flash fiction format by reading a lot of short fiction.

Second, open your mind and write with speed and boldness without significant planning. Allow your natural creativity and playfulness to emerge. Prepare to write by understanding that anything can serve as a topic for a story, and let your subconscious mind take over.

Read a lot of flash fiction

Soak up flash fiction by purchasing or borrowing some of the story collections that I've listed in the Suggested Reading section of this book. You can also go online and visit some of the flash fiction Web sites and online journals out there, such as *flashquake* or *The Vestal Review* (see Chapter 17 for Web site addresses). Read myths, urban legends, or ghost stories. Read the stories that you like over and over again to learn how they work.

If you read a lot of flash fiction, you'll discover that you naturally begin to express yourself in this format as you write.

The Flash Fiction Pool

A great way to spur your writing of flash fiction is to create a flash fiction pool. This pool is a collection of words, sentences, thoughts, and situations for writing exercises.

These topics can be about anything — words that pop into your head, interesting first lines for a story, objects that are lying on your living room floor. Do not judge any of the words or topics, just write them down and toss them into the jar. Do this for several days or weeks, jotting and tossing topics into the pool as they occur to you.

Get a collection of similar-sized, blank pieces of paper to write your topics on. I use old business cards, but you can use scraps of paper, cut-up index cards, or whatever works best for you. Next, jot down writing topics on these scraps of paper and toss them into a topic container such as a shoe box, large plastic jar, or top hat. This container should be portable and allow you to mix up the topics freely.

When you write flash fiction, your mind should be open to ideas in the world around you, and not really focused on a concrete, visual topic that you want to write about. If you feel inspired at this moment, write! Don't wait for something perfect to come along. Write about whatever comes to mind.

Flash Fiction Pool Topic Guidelines

Keep the topics short

Limit the topic description to, at most, a dozen words, or the amount of writing that can fit on the back of a business card.

Keep track of your ideas

✳ visual ✳

Make them visual and specific

Try to make the topics very specific and visual. Avoid abstract, general words, if possible. Find words that evoke an image, memory, event, or situation. Use words that help paint a picture.

Abstract	Visual
Love	Torrid passion; tender caring
Mother	Abusive Mom-of-the-Year; Earth-Mother
Sky	Wild azure air
Drink	Guzzle; chug; sip daintily

Do not judge the topic

Any topic should be fair game at this stage. Don't eliminate topics because you feel that they may be boring, inappropriate, or stupid. This is your Inner Critic talking to you, trying to sabotage your idea-generating process.

Flash Fiction Pool Topic Categories

Here are some of the categories that I commonly use when coming up with flash fiction pool topics:

Words

Select an unusual or provocative word or group of words and add it to the pool. Some of the ways you can generate these words are:

- Open the dictionary to a random page, close your eyes and pick a word

- Write down your favorite words

- Write down words that you hate

- Write down stupid words

- Write down words that make you angry

- Write down words that are fun to say

Examples: Jasmine, fecund, roly-poly, tart, felonious, bigotry, pumpkin-head, jerk, face-lift.

Add your own categories of words to this list. Explore your relationship with language and use it to boost your creative power.

Situations

Summarize a situation as a kernel for a story. This situation should get the reader involved in the story and ask herself: what is going on here?

Set up a situation that includes:

- An unusual setting

- A weird event or accident

- A universal experience (something that has happened to all of us at some point in our lives)

- A bad thing that just happened or is about to happen
- A conflict with someone or something

Examples: Lost in the woods; in the back seat of a car; first kiss; bowling love story; a fight between five-year-olds; smashed china; being awakened in the middle of the night; hiding in a cardboard box.

Characters

Introduce an unusual character to explore in the story. If you can't come up with one naturally, try some of the following techniques:

Character role and mental state

Select a list of titles and pair them with random mental states (it helps to have fun with irony here).

DETAILS

Clown	*Depressed*	
Soccer mom	*Flirtatious*	*ie) Suicidal clown*
CEO of a big company	*Obnoxious*	
Mayor	*Suicidal*	
Cheating husband	*Confused*	
Family counselor	*Sociopathic*	
Veterinarian	*Clumsy*	

Any of the words in the first list can be paired with any word in the second to create a character concept for a story. Now, put the character in a situation and begin writing.

Combine situation with character

Sometimes you see or think of something that com-
bines two otherwise unrelated images to provide
you with a story idea. This could be a trait of the
character that sparks the imagination, or a situation
that makes you curious about why this is happen-
ing and what is going to happen next.

Examples

Manic preschool teacher; absent-minded judge;
man yelling on cell phone; young mother pushing
baby stroller with a cane; superhero as a baby; man
who reads everyone else's e-mail.

Other character building ideas

- Think about the most unusual people you
  have known and describe them in a dozen
  words or less.

- Think about an actual event that happened to
  you and imagine if it happened to someone
  else you know (who'd react quite differently).
  For example: your boss, best friend, spouse, or
  someone else you know well.

Given first lines

Any line can start a story. One online publication,
The First Line (http://www.thefirstline.com/
index.htm), uses this idea for all of its story contests.
Try creating a line that:

Includes or implies immediate action

Examples: After she hit me, I...; Alex woke up in
wet grass...; The game was over...

Asks a question

Examples: Where were you last night? How did you get in here? Who did this to you?

States something unexpected or strange

Examples: An elephant ran through the trailer park...; I loved him, but he had to die...; My skull cracked on the hard wood floor...

States something to be proven or disproven

Examples: I hate you...; She is such a slut...; All men were the same...; My momma was the most evil person I ever knew...

Images

These are the easiest to come up with. Just look through old photo albums, flip though magazines and newspapers, notice interesting things in the everyday world around you.

Examples: A baby carrier in the median of a highway; an old woman mooning a truck driving by; blood pooled in the entryway; a picture of a huge family, all smiling except one young man in the back row who frowns.

Build a Pool with a Group

A flash fiction pool brings an element of randomness to your writing. When you have several minds generating unique topics, that element is enhanced.

To create a group pool, give each member 10 to 20 blank slips of paper (these can be the back of old business cards or index cards) and invite them to write down topics.

Encourage everyone to participate and add her own topics to the pool.

Once you have a good collection of writing topics, use them for group writing sessions.

Guidelines for Using the Flash Fiction Pool

Mix the topics well

Make sure that the topic you pull out of the pool is truly random.

You must write about the topic drawn

Writing on random topics helps get your creative juices flowing and encourages you to create a good story out of whatever topic is drawn from the pool.

It doesn't matter if you write alone, or with a friend or group. You must write about the topic drawn from the pool.

The words or situation on the card must appear in the story

It doesn't have to be a major part of the story, it just has to make an appearance. Be creative, weave it in somewhere unexpected or take a given line off on a bizarre tangent.

The more creative and unusual the direction your story takes, the better it will be.

Example Flash Fiction Pool

These topics were generated by one of my flash fiction classes. Feel free to use this as a starting point for your own flash fiction pool.

- 1st paycheck
- 911 or 9/11
- A superhero's first day on the job
- An accident
- An unnecessary apology
- An unwelcome visitor, with baggage
- Bad laundry
- Children
- Damn that was good!
- Damned
- Dancing babies
- Don't be afraid of your anger.
- Don't tell anyone. Please?
- Elephant
- Fate
- First time I got into a fight
- First time you had sex
- First time you lied to your parents
- Floods
- Go away!
- Graduation day

- Grandmother's funeral
- Gravy
- Hey buddy, what do you think you're doing?
- How does she do it?
- Having your identity stolen
- Hobbies
- Hot water
- Hunger as a child
- I can't believe you did that!
- I didn't kill her, at least I don't think so...
- I'm afraid I have some bad news.
- It was his/her last day on earth.
- It's broken.
- It's fake.
- Just past midnight
- Leftover
- Life in the fast lane
- Living legend
- Loneliness after breakup
- Lord, Lord
- Lost a pet
- Man, are you screwed.
- No batteries
- Nose picking
- Only one more

- Packing a suitcase (or bag) to run away
- Personal disaster
- Pets
- Please don't touch the [fill in the blank].
- Put that back where you found it.
- Quit.
- Screaming child in a four-star restaurant
- She plucked the book from the shelf and opened it.
- She went too far.
- Sold out
- Step-Mom (or Dad)
- Surprise obligation
- Take the money.
- The contents of this wastebasket
- This is your last chance.
- Toaster
- Too cheap
- Trick questions
- Trying to lose weight
- Two characters hail a taxi at the same time and neither want to give it up.
- Two green lights
- Two important people betray you.
- Uncomfortable situation

- Up on a pedestal
- We were just about to go when...
- What makes you think you can write?
- When the rain stopped
- Where do you think you're going?
- Where's the baby?
- Would you rather have your parent die or be guilty of a brutal murder and on death row?
- You might think this is perverted, but I love...
- You read an e-mail that changes your life.
- Your most angry moment

Do It!

These activities support the concepts of this chapter.

Reading

1. Read at least 20 flash fiction stories from one (or a combination of) the resources in the Suggested Reading section or in Chapter 17.

2. Select two or three of your favorite stories, reread them at least three times, and answer the following questions:

    - What did you like about it?
    - What did the author do extremely well?
    - What images or phrases in the story really stand out?

Create a Flash Fiction Pool

1. Using the techniques in this chapter, create your own flash fiction topic pool. Start with at least 25 topics. Feel free to rip off any of the example topics in this chapter to add to your own pool.

Writing Exercises

Use these exercises to practice your timed writing skills. Write for 10 minutes about each of the following topics:

1. A long-forgotten secret

2. An alcoholic in denial

3. An intelligent cat

4. An encounter with God

5. An instance of leaping before looking

First Lines

1. I don't care who you are...

2. Was that a rat I just saw?

3. Amy, put down that gun...

4. Excuse me, can you help me with...

5. The wallet was full of cash, and had a picture of my wife in it...

Quick Topics

- Never mind
- Rain
- Shaky
- Tenant
- Class

- Execution
- Up yours
- Diplomacy
- Plow
- Design

Chapter 4

Where to Get Ideas

Sometimes even when we try to do a simple thing like generating story ideas, we get stuck. Your Inner Critic gets involved in the creative process and freezes you out with the old line: "I don't know what I'm going to write about."

Don't believe it for a minute. Locked away in your mind is enough material to keep you writing for the rest of your life. You just need to know how to tap into it and use it.

Use Writing Prompts

To work around this problem, use writing prompts created by others. Here are some books with great writing prompts:

- *Fast Fiction* by Roberta Allen

- *Writing Down the Bones* and *Wild Mind: Living the Writer's Life* by Natalie Goldberg

- *The Pocket Muse* by Monica Wood

- *The Writer's Idea Book* and *The Writer's Idea Workshop* by Jack Heffron

- *The Writer's Block: 786 Ideas to Jump-Start Your Imagination* by Jason Rekulak

See Appendix B — Suggested Reading for additional details about these books.

These books provide many writing topics to get you started and help you learn how to generate topics of your own.

Tap Into Personal Experience

Your subconscious mind has already soaked up enough material for you to write about. Tap into it. It has detailed information about all of your memories, dreams, people you have known, facts and much more that can be used as raw material for your work.

You are special. You have something to write about that no one else can. Even people born in the same family see the world in radically different ways. Your voice is important and valuable. So seek it out and connect with it to write.

What are you an expert at?

Come on, I know that you are an expert at something. What do you know more about than 95% of other people? Think about it. Do you know more about bad science-fiction television of the '70s than anyone else you know? Know every statistic about your favorite pro football team for the last 50 years? Feed six kids and a golden retriever on $6,000 a year?

Your expertise is a great gateway into gathering writing ideas. Look into your professional life. What skills have you developed on the job that others see as your strengths? All jobs have highly specialized knowledge. Making Whoppers at Burger King during a lunch time rush requires skills that not everyone has. Some jobs require a great deal of technical knowledge. Are you the whiz kid that keeps the e-mail and word processors on all of the executives' laptops running? Are you the one who always deals with the difficult patients or sorts out the red tape with the HMOs?

What about your hobbies and interests? Quilting? Collecting movie posters from slasher flicks? Storm chasing? Rock climbing? Maybe you have read every one of Anne Tyler's books (even the ones she hates) and know a lot about her?

If you still are stuck, look at your childhood interests. What did you collect? Insects? Bottle caps? Coins? Did you have a passion for dinosaurs and want to be an archaeologist? An astronaut? A world-class gymnast? Some of these interests and passions may have carried over into adulthood. Use them in your writing.

Jeopardy dream categories

Here's a suggestion for generating ideas that I ran across in Douglas Coupland's *MicroSerfs*. Imagine you have been selected as a contestant on Jeopardy, and luckily the categories are your dream categories. They guarantee that you will blow out your opponents in the game. Here are mine:

- Lives of 20th century American writers
- The writing process
- Astronomy 101
- *Star Trek* (all shows)
- Creative thinking
- Pro wrestling trivia

- The care and feeding of Microsoft Word
- Corporate politics and communication
- Document design and page layout
- Sting's songs
- Cleveland Browns football, past and present
- Hot Chinese and Thai food
- Pop hits of the 80's

Your expertise lends credibility to your fiction. In fiction, if your characters are experts at skills that you have intimate knowledge of, the characters and the story will be that much more believable.

In flash fiction, this experience may translate as an industry buzzword or inside information that clearly defines a character or a situation.

Family Experiences

Your family tree can be a fertile source for fiction. Every family is filled with stories of tragedies, miracles, and everyday memories that have been told over and over. Write about family legends, eccentric relatives, and lessons you learned from family members. Don't forget your children and grandchildren. Their viewpoints and perspectives are often unique and may serve as a spark for a good story.

Consider some of these family experiences for your flash fiction:

- Accidents and tragedies
- Brushes with fame and fortune
- Relatives in trouble with the law

- How your parents/grandparents met
- Not speaking to one another
- Family jokes
- Favorite family traditions

Feels Like the First Time

The first time you experience something is usually the most memorable and interesting. These don't have to be monumental, earth-shattering experiences. Normal, everyday occurrences can be excellent fodder for flash fiction.

For example, the first time you:

- Told a lie or did something bad (original sin)
- Kissed a lover
- Felt pain
- Saw your significant other
- Gave (or witnessed) birth
- Got married
- Had sex
- Were betrayed by a friend or family member
- Drove a car
- Knew you were an adult
- Drank alcohol
- Fell in love
- Experienced the death of a loved one

Universal Experiences

There are common events that everyone experiences, yet each individual experience is unique. These experiences can be routine occurrences or life-changing moments, but each of us has these experiences at some point.

Here are a few examples of universal experiences. Can you think of others?

- The first date
- The vacation from hell
- Being pulled over by a police officer
- Moving into a new house/town/school
- Loss of innocence
- Witnessing a fight
- Being victimized
- Doing something nice for someone else
- Being bothered by a telemarketer
- Playing in the "big game"
- Getting the flu
- Recovering from an injury
- Taking a stupid chance
- Playing a practical joke
- Celebrating a birthday

Provide an Environment for Creativity

Do you do things the same way all of the time? Do you have deeply entrenched habits and routines?

New ideas don't appear unless they are nurtured and carefully grown with new experiences and fresh perspectives.

Think of ways that you can do things differently and do them often. Here are a few suggestions:

- Take a different route to work or home

- Eat at a restaurant that you never have been to before

- Read a book about a topic you know nothing about

- See a movie that you wouldn't pick unless you were dragged to go see it

- Play a practical joke on someone

- Take a class to learn something new (cooking, painting, a new language, or scuba diving.)

- Strike up a conversation with a stranger

- Take a long walk in the woods or other natural setting

What other things can you do to invite this atmosphere of creativity?

The World Around You

Simply being aware and present in the world around you can help you generate story ideas.

Reading

The newspaper is a great place to start. Maybe something intrigues you on the front page, in the crime report, in the metro section, or on the opinion page.

You can also pick up a magazine that interests you and find ideas within it. Look for stories that grab your attention and spark your writing mind.

Other media

You can find interesting characters, situations and environments for stories watching TV or surfing online. The evening newscast introduces you to the news of the day and something might catch your writer's eye. There are news magazines such as *Dateline, 20/20, 60 Minutes, 48 Hours,* and talk shows such as *Oprah, Dr. Phil, Larry King Live, Live with Regis and Kelly,* and even the *Jerry Springer Show* that may give you story ideas.

There are also entire networks devoted to every interest and type of information such as *Lifetime, CNN, Discovery, The Learning Channel,* that cover topics in depth and may ignite your imagination.

The World Wide Web has practically everything on it. Just by surfing you might meet an interesting person, gain a bit of unusual information, or encounter a story that begs you to begin writing.

Shameless voyeurism

Voyeurism? Isn't that illegal? No, I'm not talking about peeking in your neighbor's bedroom window. I'm talking about being aware of the world around you for things that might be good subjects or details for a story.

Examples:

- An interesting conversation you overhear in a checkout line or in an elevator

- An interesting person you see across the room at a restaurant

- An interesting story, rumor or bit of gossip that someone shares with you

- The quirks of a coworker

- An event you witness as a bystander (an accident, fight, argument, rescue, etc.)

Conclusion

You don't have to kill yourself looking for ideas; let them come to you. Prepare yourself for them and be open to them when they arrive. Keep a notebook with you at all times so you can capture them. You don't have to be a direct participant to write about something, you just have to have awareness to capture the ideas and use your imagination to bring them to life.

Do It!

These activities support the concepts of this chapter.

Idea Generation

Use these exercises to help generate story ideas for your flash fiction.

1.   List your own Jeopardy categories. Be sure to include six for Jeopardy, six for Double Jeopardy, and one for Final Jeopardy.

2.   List your own unique family experiences.

3.   List memorable first times in your life.

4.   List universal experiences that might be good top-
      ics for flash fiction.

5.   Pick-up a copy of a weekly magazine such as
      Newsweek, Time, People, or *U.S. News & World
      Reports* and read through it and jot down any writ-
      ing ideas you encounter.

6.   Read a daily newspaper for a week and mine as
      many ideas from it as you can.

Writing Exercises

Use these exercises to practice your timed writing skills.
Write for 10 minutes about each of the following topics:

1.   Write a story that takes place in a CEO's office

2.   A yard sale

3.   Needless stress

4.   A clueless and mean boss

5.   A parking lot altercation

First Lines

1.   He thought that he should light it on fire...

2.   A funny thing happened on the way to...

3.   I really hate it when you...

4.   When she got out of the BMW...

5.   There was a dead body in the trunk...

Quick Topics

- Apathy
- Fly
- Hatchet job
- Wrist
- Rubber ball

- Dull
- Mob
- Late night
- Dead wrong
- David

Chapter 5

Flash Writing — The First Draft

Writers are often stereotyped as masochists who do not write a line unless it springs forth fully-formed and perfect on the page. Writing the first draft can be difficult, but it doesn't have to be.

The skills necessary to write a first draft are counter-intuitive to what you may have been taught in school. Your natural writing ability has been buried under spelling rules and grammar regulations. You were taught the rules, but not how to write.

Your mind loves to play with words. It doesn't notice misspellings or dangling participles. Your subconscious mind loves to frolic with random writing topics, say bad things about other people, and create stories with brilliant bursts of imagination. The trick is to coax the playful side of your mind onto the page when you write your first draft. But, many times an Inner Critic prevents you from writing this way.

Who is this Inner Critic?

It is that inner voice that tries to protect you from making a fool out of yourself. It is more conservative than a ultra-right-wing talk show host, and very protective of the status quo. It guards its turf by belittling your attempts, censoring thoughts it deems inappropriate, and constantly bringing up spelling and grammar issues in its attempt to slow down and control the writing process.

Flash First Draft Guidelines

The following guidelines will help quiet your Inner Critic so you write freely and creatively.

Write in timed 10-minute bursts

Discipline means writing with a deadline. Deadlines for some writing projects last weeks, months, even years, but a flash fiction deadline is 10 minutes.

Use an egg timer, a watch alarm, or the timer on your microwave and set it for a 10-minute countdown. Pick a topic and write a story.

Why write in 10-minute bursts? Nothing inspires creativity like a deadline. The countdown adds pressure to your writing. This pressure doesn't give your Inner Critic time to criticize your writing, question your objectives, cross out your words, or correct your grammar.

Write fast

Speed is the important thing here. Do not let your logical, critical mind take charge of the writing process at the beginning. Writing fast gives the Inner Critic little time to react and insert itself into the writing process and tear down your first draft.

With only 10 minutes to put together a draft of an entire story, you have to write fast! Don't pause for inspiration, don't cross anything out or even think. If a word doesn't seem like exactly the one you were looking for, write down the word that is there now (or leave a blank to fill it in later) and keep going. There will be time to polish and rewrite the story later.

The important thing in this stage is to get the draft down on the page. Nothing else matters—not grammar, spelling, comma splices, or dangling participles.

Don't judge the work

When you finish a timed writing session, do not even reread the work that you've just completed. Don't let your Inner Critic convince you that what you've written is inferior, strange, or terrible. This is the first draft. The goal of this draft is just to get something down on the page, not to judge, edit, or polish your work. Write it and wait awhile before you look at it again.

Write about several topics in one session

Write on one topic and quickly move on to the next one. This allows your mind to distance itself from your work on the previous piece and accelerate the detachment process. Then, you can effectively move on to the next stage of the writing process.

Plus, if you write one stinker, you have several other chances to write something that might be pretty good. I suggest writing in three to five 10-minute blocks in one writing session.

Listen to your subconscious mind

Your subconscious mind is very powerful. Relax and write the raw words that form in your head as fast as you can. Within the subconscious mind are stored the memories of every sight, smell, sound, sensation, and every thought and feeling you have ever had. You already have the story stored in your head. Listen to it. You have to allow the thoughts

and images of your subconscious mind bubble forth
and write!

I like using random topics because they encourage
your mind to look at images and focus on thoughts
and words with no planning or preconceived objectives. This allows the story to flow.

Face your dark side

Flash writing can make you uncomfortable. You
may find yourself writing things on paper that you
never dared to say out loud. You may be afraid of
your words and what others might think about you
if they knew that you wrote this.

Common topics that make most people uncomfortable:

- Death
- Sex
- Insanity
- Fear
- Anger
- Sadness
- Self-pity
- Violence
- Selfishness
- Jealousy
- Any strong or passionate emotion

Fear is a powerful weapon of the Inner Critic. Confront these fears and write about those things that

you are uncomfortable expressing. Acknowledge the fear, but write anyway.

The dark side is an essential component of ourselves. It represents those things that we are not proud of: petty feelings of jealousy, envy, rage, and selfishness. Our dark side wants to smash dishes, punch someone in the face, flip off the driver next to you, and kick dogs and kittens. It wants to scream at your boss, cheat on your spouse, or key someone's new Porsche in the parking garage. Our dark side hates with passion and venom, and lusts with no commitment or regard for consequences.

The dark side is all of those feelings that you repress, all the harsh words left unspoken, all the destruction kept in check. It is our bad temper, selfish tears, and outlandish behavior. It is also essential for creating conflict and dramatic tension in your work. If you repress your dark side relentlessly, writing may be impossible. How are you going to get into the head of a villain, or a character about to make a disastrous mistake?

If you feel that what you have written might hurt someone, change that person's name or simply store your work in a secure place not accessible to anyone who might misunderstand your words and feelings.

Strengthen your writing by tapping into the incredible creative energy possessed by your dark side.

Understand your first draft might suck

The Inner Critic tries to convince you that your writing is crap, that the story is a waste of time, an embarrassment to you, your family, and the entire town in which you live. Ignore it. Get the words down on paper now. You can refine them later. Resist the urge to shred the paper and burn it in your trash can. These feelings pass with time and practice. Most writers hate their first drafts.

Do It!

These activities support the concepts of this chapter.

1.   Establish a dialogue with your Inner Critic. Describe it. What does it look like? What does it sound like? What strategies does it use to silence your writing? What does it say to you? Write from the critic's perspective for at least 10 minutes and be specific. Don't let your critic get the last word.

2.   What are you afraid of? What are you uncomfortable with? What are you embarrassed by? List them.

3.   Who is your shadow self (AKA your dark side)? What does he/she look like? What are his habits? Feelings? Impulses?

4.   Write about someone you hate. Surely you know someone. Tap into your hatred and let your dark side loose. Be vicious, ruthless, and totally biased and self-serving.

Writing Exercises

Use these exercises to practice your timed writing skills. Write for 10 minutes about each of the following topics:

1.   A natural disaster

2.   A lost dog

3.   A fight between two close friends

4. A dreaded Monday morning appointment

5. Write a story that takes place within a bachelor pad

First Lines

1. He's not normal...

2. Where were you last night?

3. We met at the bowling alley, and it was love at first sight...

4. He/She was the kind of person who would...

5. He admits he could have...

Quick Topics

- Earth
- Beef
- Wanted
- Alarm
- Shift

- Flunk
- Rage
- Milk
- Mood lighting
- Streaking

Chapter 6

Preparing Your Ideas

Now, you have a great idea, but is it good for a flash fiction story? The topic is ripe for exploration, but maybe too big to tackle in a flash fiction format. You might need to prepare the idea for flash fiction before you write.

Narrow your focus

Take the topic and break it down into tiny, manageable tasks.

In Anne Lamott's bestselling book about writing, *Bird by Bird*, she suggests creating your own one-inch picture frame, and looking at the world with this small window. Through this picture frame, you realize that you only see a small part of the whole picture, and as a result, your topic becomes easier to write about.

Find an image or scene

Take a big subject such as a main character or a tragic event, condense it using a smaller image or part of the story. If the topic is the death of a parent, use an image or scene to illustrate how the character feels about the event. For example, try these images or scenes:

- The phone call in the middle of the night
- Picking out a casket

- Trying to write a eulogy
- Remembering the last argument you had with your parent

Keep the scene focused in one area within one image.

If you are looking at a deadly auto crash, do not focus on the accident as a whole, but pick out and write about one detail to represent the whole. For example:

- A burnt and twisted stop sign
- A puddle of blood on the double-yellow line
- A shredded tire and piece of twisted metal
- The emergency lights from the ambulances and police cruisers lighting up the nightmarish scene

Write about a moment in time

Choose a moment in time and write about that moment. Not just any moment, but that single moment that changes everything forever — where the littlest choice you make, a single bad decision, a choice to go or stay, a wrong turn has a significant and permanent impact on character.

These are often the little choices that you make that seem so innocent at the time, but often become the things that you rejoice in or regret forever. In other moments in time, fate hands you something that changes your life forever, leaving you to deal with it.

What are some of these?

- Discovering that you have brain cancer
- Losing a finger or toe
- Having one too many drinks before getting behind the wheel of a car
- Showing up late for work on the wrong day
- Losing your temper at an airport
- Scaring someone
- Kissing someone who isn't your spouse

These are great moments to focus on when writing flash fiction. These moments are immediate, are engorged with conflict, and can create a story just in the writing.

Limit the scene

In other words, put the story in a box. Trap the characters together in a place where they can't escape from each other (or themselves) until they resolve the conflict between them.

Here are some limited scenes:

- A cabin in the woods during a raging storm
- Trapped in an elevator
- In a closet, as the result of winning spin-the-bottle, for seven minutes in heaven
- A police interrogation room
- A jury deliberation chamber
- Two characters handcuffed together

Make an abstract topic concrete

This is part of showing vs. telling. Select a general, abstract topic and bring it to life. Here are some examples of abstract topics:

- Obsessive love

- Extreme vanity

- The constant victim

- A bully

- A place no one wants to be

- An unloved child

Now find a way to illustrate this topic for a story. Think about how you would illustrate obsessive love in a visual, concrete way.

- Maybe the story can be about a woman who ignores her husband because of her obsessive love for winning ribbons and trophies with her springer spaniel, Trixie.

- Maybe the obsessive love is between two co-workers who write each other about their idealized love via online chat rooms, but they do not know that the person in the cube next to them is the object of their affection and they despise each other in real life.

Do It!

These activities support the concepts of this chapter.

1. Make yourself a one-inch picture frame by cutting a one-inch square in the middle of an index card. Take it with you to a place (it can be anyplace) and look through it for at least 10 minutes and write about what you see.

Idea Generation

Use these exercises to help generate story ideas for your flash fiction.

1. Create an image or a scene that illustrates these bigger events:

    *   An abusive relationship

    *   First love

    *   Death of a child

    *   A feud between family members

    *   A heroic act

2. List additional moments in time that might be good content for a flash fiction story. Do this for at least 10 minutes.

3. In 10 minutes, list settings that confine the characters in the story. Think of boxes, confining situations, or stage set of a play. Be creative here.

4. Illustrate the abstract topics listed below:

    *   Unrequited love

    *   Someone who is bored in a dangerous situation

- Fight between friends
- A cowardly act
- Rescue

Writing Exercises

Use these exercises to practice your timed writing skills. Write for 10 minutes about each of the following topics:

1. A 15-year-old boy trying to impress a 15-year-old girl

2. A 13-year-old girl trying to impress a 13-year-old boy

3. Someone talking his/her way out of trouble

4. Running out of gas

5. Falling asleep during an important meeting

First Lines

1. That was for losers...

2. Can I leave now?

3. What was he doing there?

4. There were bats in the attic. Hundreds of them...

5. I stepped on the cat and...

Quick Topics

- Pinch me
- Lost
- Etch A Sketch
- Poop
- Psychic

- Clear blue
- Cheesecake
- Nose dive
- Relocation
- Bikini

Chapter 7

Character Guidelines

The reader identifies with the characters in a piece, so characters are an essential part of fiction. In flash fiction, you must develop and describe your characters in very few words. Make the most of your opportunities. Show the character in action. Describe the little details about him that brings him to life in the reader's mind. One little detail or action can show us a lot about who the character is.

No boring characters

Why would anyone want to read about a boring character? Most people read fiction to escape from their "boring" lives. Characters must have interesting jobs, hobbies, ideas or be involved in interesting situations. Readers can also identify with characters that are likeable or have a quirky outlook on life.

Why do you think that detective and police procedural novels are so popular? Only a small percentage of people are involved in law enforcement, medicine, and the legal system, yet our shelves are filled with detective stories and medical and legal thrillers. How about fantasy, science-fiction, and romance novels? What is their appeal? All of these stories take us away from our mundane, everyday lives, and take us to a world we may know little or nothing about except through the author's eyes.

This doesn't mean that all interesting stories must involve trigger-happy cops and cowboys, wealthy heiresses in designer gowns, generous doctors or lawyers.

Good fiction can be about ordinary characters facing extraordinary circumstances. These might be problems we identify with, or ones that we hope to never have to face. As writers, we must make the reader root for the character to triumph over the obstacles in her path.

No perfect characters

No one is perfect. A reader can't identify with a perfect character. A hero who cannot fail or is never in danger is not interesting. Neither is an all-powerful villain who, having no visible flaws or weaknesses, can only be defeated by luck or circumstance alone.

There is no such thing as a perfect murder. Every crime scene has evidence. Every plan has a flaw. Every person has a weakness that is exploited at some time.

No stereotypical characters

Hollywood has beaten many character types into the ground. In flash fiction, there is no room for them. As a writer, you must paint a realistic picture of an interesting character. Here are some examples of stereotypical characters:

- The noble knight
- The vengeful, angry other woman
- The gay hairdresser

- The African-American drug dealer
- The teenage punk skateboarder
- The jolly fat storekeeper
- The absent-minded professor

You've seen all of these before, time and time again, in movies you rent from Blockbuster.

Clichéd characters are a common flaw in fiction, and writing good fiction avoids clichés.

The character must change

The reader expects change in the story. The story gives us a glimpse into what may be the most important event that has ever taken place in this character's life, and a change will occur. It could be a physical change, an emotional change, or a change in the character's attitude. Maybe the character doesn't change at all, but the failure to change allows the reader to see the character in a different way.

This change could be for the better or worse, but it is always significant.

Do It!

These activities support the concepts of this chapter.

1.   List several characters that may have "boring" lives. Next to them, list at least three events or actions that would make these lives interesting.

2.   List as many character clichés that you can think of in 10 minutes.

3.   From the clichés on this list, choose one and give it a creative twist to make it fresh and interesting.

Writing Exercises

Use these exercises to practice your timed writing skills. Write for 10 minutes about each of the following topics:

1.   A spider spinning a web

2.   A game that has been knocked onto the floor

3.   Unrealistic enthusiasm about a lottery ticket

4.   A careless act

5.   Mistaken identity

First Lines

1.   In the bedroom...

2.   I can just imagine...

3.   We've got you covered...

4.   I won't date a guy/gal who...

5.   You will survive...

Quick Topics

- Basketball
- Dwarf
- Canoe
- Night out
- Thumbs up

- Migraine
- Rock star
- Cafeteria
- Yellow
- Poor

Chapter 8

Sources of Character

A character in flash fiction doesn't need to be developed in as much detail as one in longer fiction, but your character must be believable within the word limits of a flash fiction story. So where do you find character ideas for flash fiction? In one or more of these four places:

- The past
- The present
- Your imagination
- Books and periodicals

The Past

Each person comes into the world with a cast of characters already in place in his life: parents, siblings, aunts, uncles, cousins, grandparents, all with unique habits and eccentricities that make them memorable.

Outside of the family, you had friends, neighbors, classmates, teachers, members of churches or organizations that you interacted with growing up.

As an adult, you have professors, roommates, bosses, coworkers and members of the community to draw character ideas from.

Remember these individuals and try to recollect specific details that can be written about. Who are these people in your life?

Here are some examples of people to write about:

- The class bully
- Your first love
- Your favorite relative
- The outcast of the family
- Your first roommate
- Your first boss

The Present

Public observation

Go to a public place such as a restaurant, library, park, or mall, and jot down details about the people you see.

- **What are they doing?** Talking on a cell phone? Looking around aimlessly? Dashing through the mall being chased by mall security? Looking bored? Excited? Angry?

- **What is the most noticeable thing about this person?** A low-cut, ruby-sequined blouse? A waxed handle-bar mustache? A lime-colored T-shirt that says Boys are Stupid? A huge wart on his nose?

- **What objects are visible around them or on them?** Visible objects can tell us a lot about an individual, about what he values and how he feels about himself. What do these items say

about a character? A toy Star Wars light saber?
A book of poems by Sharon Olds? A money
clip? A Burger King crown? Crutches? A half-
moon belly-button piercing?

Hone your powers of observation and jot down
notes for as many people as you can.

Photographs

Take a photograph from a newspaper or magazine,
select a person in the photo, and describe what you
see. Can this be a character for your fiction?

Imagination

Creative Alteration

Place yourself or other people you know well in an
extraordinary situation. How would you react if
you were abducted by aliens? Came face-to-face
with a serial killer? Experienced a fire that
destroyed everything you own? Afflicted with a ter-
minal illness? Imagine creative scenarios of your
own to add to this list.

You can also alter characters that you have
described or people you know with a few "what if"
questions. What if your boss was secretly a million-
aire? A confused KGB agent? A man pretending to
be a woman?

Creative Borrowing

Start with characters from other places, such as
books, television and movies, and change them subtly by asking a few "what if" questions.

Examples

- How would the Star Wars saga have been different if Darth Vader were female? "Luke. I'm your mama Luke. Search your feelings... ." Yikes!

- What if Ahab had been a custodian at a local school building instead of the captain of a ship? What would be his "great white whale" to fulfill his need for vengeance?

You can also borrow a character that you find in a current event or magazine article or hear about from somebody else, and put that character in the middle of the action.

Books and Periodicals

Read actively for new ideas for characters and details that may help develop exciting ones. Newspapers and magazines are filled with memorable people, and well-written personality profile pieces.

Reading fiction introduces us to interesting characters that we want to know more about or inspires the creation of new characters.

Do It!

These activities support the concepts of this chapter.

1. List 10 to 20 memorable characters from your past; jot down a few details you remember about them.

2. Make a quick list of 10 to 25 people that you interact with in your life almost daily, not people that you know intimately, just people you see often. Co-workers, the mailman, the checkout clerk at your

favorite store, a waitress at a restaurant you frequently visit, or other people. Write down the most memorable thing about them, and list a few facts that you know about them through observation and interaction.

3. Go to a public place and, following the guidelines in the *Public Observation* section, create details about three of the people you see, and make up a story about them.

4. Take a real-life person (or a favorite character from a book, TV show or movie) and ask "what if" questions about this person. Ask 20 or more questions and see what interests you most about her.

5. Begin a photo file. Seek out interesting photos in magazines, newspapers, and online. Add these photos to your own collection and put them in a file to use as future writing prompts.

6. Begin a character file. Clip profile pieces of unusual people out of newspapers and magazines and keep them in a file. Save interesting facts about people, essays, or anything else that grabs your attention.

Writing Exercises

Use these exercises to practice your timed writing skills. Write for 10 minutes about each of the following topics:

1. An unwanted visit

2. A stupid argument

3. A creepy character

4. An annoying person

5. An angry customer

First Lines

1. It was a lot of fun...

2. We need to fill in a few blanks...

3. Don't have a cow...

4. Isn't that the point?

5. We'll be there...

Quick Topics

- Deep red
- Poor
- Breakfast
- Slash
- Cockroach

- Scaling
- Cat
- Push-up
- Tongue
- Adapt

Chapter 9

Creating Characters for Flash Fiction

In flash fiction, you don't have a lot of space to flesh out a fully formed character, so you have to use words and actions frugally.

Description

Physical description is not as important in flash fiction as it is in short stories or novels. Give the reader a few details and let her imagination do the rest of the work. To help the reader visualize the character, ask yourself the following questions:

- What is the first thing you notice about this character when you see him/her?

- What physical attributes or imperfections make this character stand out?

  Try to limit this to no more than three details, and show these through action or dialogue within the story itself.

- What does this character do if you observe him for a while?

  Does he look at his watch nervously? Adjust his tie? Tap his foot impatiently?

- What type of body language does this character have?

- How does he feel about his body?

Possessions

Possessions indicate the character's attitude toward material things. Possessions can also be a strong motivation for a character.

- What does the character have?

  Houses, vehicles, high-ticket item home electronics, power tools, weapons, just to name a few examples.

- What possessions are important to her?

- What possessions are unimportant?

Use possessions to give the reader clues about the setting of the story or to indicate something important about the character.

Personality

Personality tells the reader about the character's outlook and attitude toward the world.

- What type of person is she? What is her outlook on the world?

  Is she depressed? Comfortable and happy? Enraged? Bitter? Giddy? Is she the sort of person who must avenge every little wrong? Or the sort of person who never fights back and is an eternal victim?

- What actions or details can you include that will bring out this personality?

  Show personality through interactions with other characters, actions she takes, body language, and thoughts versus actions.

  Don't tell us that she is vengeful. Show us how she gets even with the rude customer service clerk at the laundromat. Let the reader witness these actions and judge them for herself.

Flaws/Shortcomings

No one likes perfect characters. We don't trust them. We don't believe them. Ask yourself, what is the major weakness that the character has to work very hard to overcome? (If the character can overcome it at all?) This is often called a fatal flaw. Some example fatal flaws:

- Greed — The character values money above all other things including relationships with family.

- Lust — She is happily married, but is willing to throw it all away in a fling with a co-worker.

- Ignorance —He doesn't know his girlfriend is a foreign spy.

- Mental illness — She has a severe case of bipolar disorder and refuses to do anything about it.

Let's face it. She can't simply have flawless skin, fit easily into a size 2 dress, have the perfect job as a criminal law attorney, and be married to a handsome personal trainer who adores her. She must have a weakness. Weaknesses make the character come to life. They make us believe she's real and help us feel connected to the character.

Maybe the perfect skin is due to thousands of dollars worth of cosmetic surgery, the size 2 because she's bulimic, and the personal trainer may act as if he adores her, but he is sleeping with all of his clients.

A perfect story is one where the character faces a situation that forces her to confront her fatal flaw.

Secrets/Skeletons in the closet

Are you having trouble coming up with a fatal flaw? Give your character a sinister secret. What is the secret that the character wants to keep hidden? Some examples:

- He has a child with another woman, but has told no one.
- She suffers from severe manic-depression.
- He hates his mother-in-law.
- She embezzles a little money from work when she gets the chance.

What will the character do to keep this dirty little secret hidden? How far will he go? Lie? Cheat? Steal? Kill?

These secrets can be used to help develop motivation, or intensify a conflict already present within the story.

Redeeming quality

Every character has a strength that makes him likable and makes the reader root for him. The redeeming quality is often the strength the character uses to overcome the fatal flaw.

Example redeeming qualities

- Is kind to animals

- Follows a strict code of honor

- Will not abandon or betray friends at any cost

- Loves his spouse and will make great sacrifices to protect her

But don't forget about the villain of the story. Even the worst, nastiest bad guy can't be all bad. Find something that makes the monster a bit human to make the reader care (even if just a little bit) about what happens to him. After all, Norman Bates had a deep love of his mother. Hannibal Lecter only eats those who fail to adhere to his rigid code of honor. Darth Vader sacrificed power, victory, and his life to save Luke from being killed by the Emperor. What redeeming qualities does your character have?

Motivation

To paraphrase the *American Heritage Dictionary — Fourth Edition*:

> *motivation: To provide with an incentive; move to action; impel.*

What does this character want?

Everyone wants something. Some people want money. Others want love. Some want a shiny new red Ford Freestar minivan. Look deep into your character's mind and pull out what she wants more than anything else in the world. That is motivation.

Obstacles

Now that you know what your character wants, create ways to prevent him from getting it.

So what barriers, challenges, or opposition must the character face to fulfill her needs? Use the character's fatal flaws and redeeming qualities to create these obstacles in your story. These don't always have to be earthshaking, life or death struggles, just interesting enough to write a story.

Some obstacles might be:

- Another character opposes the character and tries to prevent her from reaching her objectives.

- The character doesn't have the resources (for example, money, skills, persuasion) to achieve her objective.

- The character is thrust into an unfamiliar situation.

- The character is faced with a situation where taking the wrong action (or inaction) causes great harm to herself or others.

- The character is forced to deal with her greatest fear.

For example, a character who is deathly afraid of heights, but will also sacrifice anything for the good of his family, must climb out onto the ledge of an eight-story building to prevent his despondent 13-year-old son from jumping.

Do It!

These activities support the concepts of this chapter.

1. Using the character creation guidelines in this chapter, create a character by answering all of the questions as completely as possible.

2. From your reading, list the fatal flaws of your favorite characters from literature or film. Next, find redeeming qualities for those same characters.

3. List some things that could be considered to be skeletons in the closet.

Writing Exercises

Use these exercises to practice your timed writing skills. Write for 10 minutes about each of the following topics:

1. An immovable object versus an irresistible force

2. A terrible secret

3. A noticeable scar

4. A generous act from an evil person

5. A misguided cause

First Lines

1. Once you know your...
2. Happily ever after?
3. If only...
4. I want you...
5. Is there anything else?

Quick Topics

- Debt
- Burning
- Boo-boo
- Coleslaw
- Paint

- Age 13
- Shorts
- Toxic
- Dilate
- Grave

Chapter 10

Description

Good description is stealthy. It sneaks up on you and surprises you when you least expect it. It slowly paints a picture for you, one small stroke at a time, and eventually you stand back and appreciate the entire masterpiece. Yet good description is difficult to write. Too much detail and you bore the reader by telling him everything that he should be seeing, hearing, feeling, and thinking. Too little detail, the reader gets confused and doesn't have enough information to engage the imagination to help fill in the blanks. How do you create good description that strikes a balance between the two extremes?

Be an observer

Pay attention to the world around you. Watch what happens at the office, restaurant, or mall. Listen to conversations. Focus on the first thing that grabs your attention when you enter a room. What is the most interesting thing that you see? Act as if you are witnessing a crime. You have to remember every detail in the scene so you can help the police later.

Slow down and notice the world around you. Note the taste and texture of your baloney sandwich with honey mustard and the thoughts that this taste and texture evoke. Listen to the ambient noise in the office around you. What do you hear? Practice honing your perceptions to improve your observation.

Be a better listener

We spend so much of our lives flooded with auditory stimuli. We start our morning with a blast of sound from our alarm clock, go through our days attached to conference calls, cell phones, TV, and radio everywhere we go. Conversations are now anxiety-driven events where we no longer listen, but wait for our next chance to jump in and speak.

Practice reflective listening

Reflective listening is commonly used in counseling and psychotherapy, and it is an essential skill for the serious writer.

When someone speaks to you, take a moment to process what has been said and repeat it back by starting with a statement along the lines of: "What you are telling me is..." or "Let me see if I understand you correctly, you said that..."

Listening reflectively forces you to listen to the conversation and does not allow you to plan your response as the other person speaks. If you don't understand what the speaker said, ask questions to help clarify the speaker's words.

Focus on a specific aspect each day

One way to be observant is to make a conscious effort to focus on one aspect of your life each day. Choose an aspect that might be drowned out in the flood of stimuli that engulf you each day. For example:

Colors — Select a color such as red, purple, or yellow and make an effort to notice everything that you see of that color today.

Objects or Shapes— Choose a common object that you will look for today, such as eyes, churches, wheels, or doors. You can also do this with shapes— triangles, ovals, diamonds, and rectangles. When was the last time you even paid attention to the shapes around you?

Sounds — Be aware of a specific sound that occurs in everyday life. Laughter, drum beats in music, traffic sounds, the sound of air, water, or any other sound.

Light and Weather — Observe light during the day, indoor and outdoor. Notice shadows and lack of light. Consciously notice the weather on a given day, the clouds, breezes, and how they change from dawn until midnight.

Nature — Choose a part of nature to pay close attention to today. Birds, for example, or a type of tree, flower, or bug.

Notice language

Language is the tool of your trade.

Be aware of the language in your life and how you, and others, use it. Focus on the common oral and written catch phrases your kids, parents, and co-workers use.

Take time to focus on a specific aspect of language for the day. For example:

Parts of speech — Such as verbs, nouns, adverbs, adjectives, or prepositional phrases.

Clichés — Are everywhere, on billboards, in magazines, and in TV commercials.

A classification of words — Words used to describe nature or color, swear words and insults, sexual words (and words twisted to have sexual innuendo), business jargon, techno-babble, slang, or words that have several meanings.

Select one of these classifications of words to look and listen for each day. In your notebook, list those you encounter.

Use all of your senses

Most writers exist in a single dimension, describing the visual aspect of the scene, sometimes incorporating sound into the work. But writers often overlook smell, taste, and touch. When describing a scene or a character, be sure to engage all of the senses wherever possible.

Be specific

Use the most concrete, visual language possible. The right word forms a picture in the reader's mind.

Use strong, vivid, precise language to communicate your ideas. Use descriptive adjectives, solid nouns, and strong action verbs. Use a good thesaurus to help you find that perfect word.

Examples

Non-specific	Specific
Red	Ruby, blood, crimson, magenta
Flower	Long-stemmed red rose, African violet, dandelion, marigold, sunflower, tulip
Car	Mustang GT convertible, Chevy Cavalier, Lexus, Mini Cooper, Saab wagon
Eat	Nibble, consume, wolf, pick at

See how the right word makes all the difference? I highly recommend J.I. Rodale's *Synonym Finder*, which could well become one of your most useful resources.

Use resources

Use plant and wildlife identification manuals to help you define the natural world around you. This helps you move away from vague language. Writing has more power if it is specific, especially if you can call every bird, plant, tree, rock, star, and flower by name.

Go to the library and pick up these types of books. Name the trees and wildflowers in your yard and at the park. Identify the rocks in your driveway and the stars up in the sky. Naming things precisely gives you power.

Show, don't tell

Sometimes getting specific doesn't mean simply using the right word, but describing a scene. Show the reader sadness instead of telling him about it. Describe it without even using the word sad itself.

If you are writing about an abstraction such as love, joy, hate, or sadness, try to create seven or more concrete images that evoke this abstraction.

Focus on an image or incident that illustrates the abstraction

Don't tell the reader that the family was dysfunctional, show her the dead-silent Thanksgiving dinner where no one says a word.

Don't tell us that the man was ugly, show us how babies cry when he looks at them, how adults studiously avoid looking at him because they don't want to be rude and stare, and how they hush children from making a comment about the man as he walks by.

Do It!

These activities support the concepts of this chapter.

1.   Think up 10 to 12 more specific words for the following vague words:

   - Grass

   - Tree

   - Rock

   - Leader

   - Restaurant

   - Alcohol

   - Sport

2.   Pick a particular sense or dimension of your life that you are going to be more aware of today.

3. Select a classification of words that you are going to focus on being more aware of this week, and write down these words in your notebook as you encounter them.

4. Create an image or a scene that illustrates these bigger events:

    - An abusive relationship

    - First love

    - Death of a child

    - A feud between family members

    - A heroic act

Writing Exercises

Use these exercises to practice your timed writing skills. Write for 10 minutes about each of the following topics:

1. An unhappy marriage

2. A guilty woman

3. A man making a difficult decision

4. A sad, lonely place

5. A person faking happiness

First Lines

1. You won't believe who called me...

2. I just feel...

3. Attention shoppers...

4. Who got away?

5. What are you doing tonight?

Quick Topics

- Liquid
- Waste
- Sweat
- Kitchen mess
- Nose

- Flex
- Deed
- Hotshot
- Hurricane
- Mirror

Chapter 11

Point of View and Setting

Point of View

First-Person

All stories with a first-person point of view (POV) use the word "I" to tell the story.

You always know who is telling the story, even if that character is unreliable. The story is told subjectively. You have free access to the narrator's thoughts, and you can use bad grammar, slang, and everyday language, if this is how the narrator speaks.

Many flash fiction stories are told using this POV. Most of the stories in the Story Examples section of this book use it.

Third-Person POV

The third-person POV uses "he" and "she" instead of "I." It can be used like a first-person POV, limiting the narrative to one perspective, or allow the author to tell a story from several different characters' perspectives. Most bestselling novels use a third-person POV.

M.K. Hobson's story "Ice Cream" uses the third-person POV.

Omniscient vs. Limited

In the omniscient or "all-knowing" POV, the thoughts and feelings of all of the characters are known to the reader. The reader can jump from mind to mind without restriction. The omniscient POV can be very confusing for a reader, as well as kill any suspense that might be present in the story. The omniscient POV is rarely used in fiction at all, and in flash fiction in particular. Two books that use it are *The French Lieutenant's Woman* by John Fowles and, more recently, *The Lovely Bones* by Alice Sebold.

The limited POV is the most common POV in novel-length fiction today. A limited POV has full access to the thoughts and feelings of a single character at one time. Many novels have several different third-person-limited narrators.

Second-Person POV

Tells the story as if the reader participates in it. It uses the word "you," is told in the present tense, and often sounds insistent and forceful. The second-person POV is rarely used, but commands immediate attention.

The stories "Tomato" and "The Shelf Life of Faceless Dolls and New Men" both use the second-person POV.

Setting

The setting of a story establishes where and when the story takes place.

In flash fiction, you must establish the where and when in the story in as few words as possible.

Location

Location fixes a character to a specific place. Where is this story taking place? Does the character fit in this environment? If not, why?

Building this specific place is often as simple as adding a few descriptive details.

In M.K. Hobson's "Ice Cream," the protagonist tells us, by using specific details, what the environment feels like to her.

> *She sits in a tepid bathtub, knees to chin. The tub is deeper than it is wide; it's like bathing in a drinking glass.*
>
> *She meets Brendan at a stand bar that's the size of a Greyhound bus-station bathroom.*
>
> *She sits hunched over a plate-sized table to keep from knocking her head on a low-hanging styrofoam lobster.*

Hobson never has to tell us that her protagonist is uncomfortable in her environment. We feel it through her words and metaphors that this environment is not ideal for this character and her major motivation is to get relief from it.

In Charles Tuomi's "I Hope He Likes It" the setting is revealed gradually, adding details that slowly assemble a picture for the reader. With about 30 words left in the story, he reveals that it is taking place on a train in a station where the conductor is checking ticket stubs. This revelation makes perfect sense with all of the details that have been subtly presented throughout the story.

Creating location

Use details that are unique to a particular environment. Describe the objects in the story that help the reader figure out where you are, through the details alone.

You can say it directly

"She is too big for her apartment." M. K. Hobson's "Ice Cream"

"It's Two-Minute Date night at this bar that you hate..." Clint Meadows' "Tomato"

But even though the setting is stated directly, it is fleshed-out further through descriptive details woven throughout the entire story.

Using location-specific references

There are many different ways you can establish the location of your story using few words.

Does it take place indoors or outdoors?

Use clear indicators such as weather, nature, or temperature for outdoor scenes. Other criteria that determine the location, the quality of light (day or night), windows, doors, and objects that are usually only found outdoors (for example, flag poles, bulldozers, boulders, or mountains).

Nature specific to a place

You don't find palm trees outdoors in Ohio, but in Los Angeles, they are everywhere. Know what the soil looks like in the location of the story. Is it sand-colored, brown, or red? What are the species of birds that live in the area? Look for unusual details about the place where the story occurs.

If your story takes place in a specific state or area of the state, use the proper names of other towns, rivers, roads, and landmarks to establish the location.

Objects specific to a location

If your story takes place in a school, ask yourself, what things do you normally see, hear, and smell in a school?   Take the time to create an inventory of these things, and then find logical locations to insert them into the story.

Time

The date and time of the story helps provide a sense of realism. While it isn't as important as other details in flash fiction stories, it still has a place.

Stopping time

There are several ways that you can establish the time that your story takes place.

State it directly — John Steinbeck's story "How Mr. Hogan Robbed a Bank"starts like this:

> *On the Saturday before Labor Day, 1955, at 9:04 1/2*
> *A.M., Mr. Hogan robbed a bank.*

Use cultural references — such as TV shows, books, music, popular personalities of the era that the story takes place in.

Use historical events — We all remember where we were when the planes plunged into the World

Trade Center, when John F. Kennedy was assassi-
nated, when Neil Armstrong took his first steps on
the moon, when the Challenger exploded. Historical events and figures tend to be touchstones for our
most vivid memories. Use historic times, people,
and events to solidify the time in your stories.

Do It!

These activities support the concepts of this chapter.

Point-of-View

1.   Write a story using the first-person POV.

2.   Rewrite that same story using the third-person
      POV.

3.   Rewrite the story a third time using the second-
      person POV. Which one do you like best? Why?

Setting

1.   Write about your childhood home using details to
      establish the setting.

2.   Write a story that takes place during a famous
      event or period in history.

3.   Write a story that takes place in the following set-
      tings, but don't state the "where" directly. Use
      details and description to establish the scenes.

      • High school

      • An abandoned factory

      • In the distant future

      • 19th century log cabin

Writing Exercises

Use these exercises to practice your timed writing skills. Write for 10 minutes about each of the following topics:

1.   A birthday party from the following POVs:

    • The 6-year-old who is having the birthday.

    • A teenaged boy in love with the girl he brought to the party.

    • The girl who is with the boy, but doesn't love him and wants to ask if they can just be friends.

    • The workaholic dad of the birthday boy.

    • The doting, yet dissatisfied mom of the birth-day boy.

    • An 90-year-old man who knows that this is the last party he will ever attend in his life.

First Lines

1.   I admit it...

2.   They hit it off...

3.   You got caught...

4.   Go to hell...

5.   Where did they find him?

Quick Topics

- Inside scoop
- Superiority
- Sunburn
- Suck
- Cane

- Test
- Root
- Workaholic
- Cheese
- Freezer

Chapter 12

Event and Conflict

Flash fiction has an event, which is a moment, a scene into which we are thrust. In flash fiction, you have to get from point A to point B in as little time as possible. Usually the writer has to focus on one scene at a time and use words carefully to enhance the event and conflict.

Characteristics of Event for Flash Fiction

Keep it simple. Flash fiction doesn't have room for complicated, information-rich plots. It only has room for a single incident or event.

Use the following guidelines to help create an event for flash fiction:

- Flash fiction rarely has subplots or parallel plots. There isn't enough room.

- Many flash fiction stories are told in the present tense and avoid flashback wherever possible.

- The story begins in the middle of the action, as close to the climax as possible.

Conflict

Conflict is essential to good fiction of any length. If there is no conflict, there is no change (see below). Conflict makes the story interesting and forces the change to happen. Conflict occurs when two forces oppose each other within the story. There are four basic types of conflict:

- Character vs. Character
- Character vs. Self
- Character vs. Society
- Character vs. Nature

Character vs. Character

This is the simplest form of conflict — two characters want the same thing. The same woman, a ten dollar bill lying in the street, the same job, the good hammer in the toolbox, or the last bottle of Liquid Tide on sale.

Character vs. Self

This character is struggling with a decision. She faces a choice. The decision she makes must have a consequence. The character's conscience prevents or encourages an action. For example:

- To cheat on a lover
- To steal a pack of gum
- To shoot the neighbor's cat

Character vs. Society

This character is going against the grain, standing out in a crowd, and resisting the severe pressure to conform, be nice, do what he is told. This character is facing tremendous odds to achieve his goal.

Character vs. Environment

This character is fighting for his life and the world around him is the enemy. He could be lost in a jungle, pinned underneath a wrecked tractor, or trapped in a jail cell. These types of conflict are usually fights for survival.

Intensifying Conflict

The number one reason that readers lose interest in a story is that it does not have enough conflict or the stakes for the conflict are not high enough.

Make the stakes extremely high. One of these characters has to lose something. The more important that something is, the higher the stakes. Failure should cause one of the following consequences:

- Death or serious injury

- Serious financial hardship

- A damaged relationship, a divorce, loss of love or respect from an important person

- Damage or loss of an important object — a wallet, a priceless Picasso painting, a favorite stuffed frog

- Loss of reputation or respect within the community or within himself

- Set in motion an undesirable series of events — an IRS audit, an arrest warrant, the notice of an organized crime boss

- Change in attitude toward herself — Loses self-respect, is resigned to suffer in a bad situation, or goes along just to get along

Conflict in flash fiction should ALWAYS have extremely high stakes!

Raising the stakes

This can be done in one of the following two ways:

- The cost of failure gets higher as the story progresses.

- The problem gets worse as a result of the character's attempts to resolve it.

Do It!

These activities support the concepts of this chapter.

Event

1. Create a story that begins in the middle of the following events:

    - A prank gone horribly wrong

    - A bad first date

    - A shotgun wedding

    - An alien landing

    - An encounter with a dangerous creature

Conflict

1. List at least 5 stories (these can be novels, short stories, or movies) that demonstrates each type of conflict.

    - Character vs. Character

    - Character vs. Self

    - Character vs. Society

    - Character vs. Environment

2. List at least 10 ways that a current problem you are dealing with in your life can get worse.

Writing Exercises

Use these exercises to practice your timed writing skills. Write for 10 minutes about each of the following topics:

1. A rivalry between two high-school students

2. An incident that ends in violence

3. Two people having a polite disagreement about something very important

4. A bad situation gets a whole lot worse

5. Soldiers on a battlefield

First Lines

1. I knew that you couldn't be trusted...

2. Honey, I'm home...

3. I have to have...

4. Don't do this. It's not worth it...

5. He found the body in the kitchen...

Quick Topics

- Algebra
- Nap
- Inside scoop
- Psycho
- Munchies

- Fetch
- Spin the bottle
- Waste
- Chump change
- Bass

Chapter 13

Style

Flash fiction is unique because it is not bound by the conventional rules of longer fiction. It isn't poetry, but many writers use it as a prose extension of the poetic form.

Flash fiction writers, like poets. choose words that build images and evoke feelings in the reader.

Flash fiction can be surreal use a unique format or word choices to present an interesting mood or style for a story.

Creating Style

There are many ways to create style in flash fiction:

- Word count
- Genre
- Topic
- Format
- Weirdness

Word count

The word count of a story influences the style of the writing. Many markets and contests have strict guidelines on word count, usually encouraging the stories to be less than a specific number of words.

Some of these markets and contests require that you have the exact number of words in a story, no more and no less.

Example

The 55 Fiction Contest, held by the *New Times SLO* publication, requires the entries to have fewer than 55 words.

Genre

Flash fiction comes in nearly every genre available to longer fiction. Science fiction, erotic, and horror flash fiction are going to have a different feel than traditional or literary flash fiction. They use different words, lingo, and images.

Reading science fiction, we are not surprised by purple soil, piss-yellow sky, or intelligent pools of lime Jell-O that speak to the hero.

When reading horror, we are not shocked by the vampire chained to the basement wall, surrounded by a ring of minced garlic.

When reading erotica, we are not shocked by the nakedness and brazen nature of the characters. That is what we expect when we pick up one of these stories. Genre can have a significant impact on the style of your flash fiction.

Topic

Style driven by a topic often influences the content of the story.

Some markets or contests provide the writer with a topic to write about (for example, revenge, mistaken identity, or drinking coffee.) or might even include specific words and lines that must be included in the piece somewhere.

Example

At *The First Line* (www.thefirstline.com), the editors, and at times the readers, select a line to begin a story. According to the editors, the goal is "to see how many different directions we can take when we start from the same place."

Format

Some writers create style in a story by writing it in a unique form.

Write the story in the format of:

- A will or legal document
- As e-mail correspondence
- Journal entries
- Instructions for an object
- Phone or voice-mail messages
- Television commercial
- Dialogue between fictional characters

Have fun with different forms. Do not limit yourself to traditional, neatly organized paragraphs. Get creative! Create a story out of a ransom note, a personal ad, the entry in a *TV Guide* listing, or the message on a billboard overlooking a highway.

Weirdness

In the tradition of magical realism and the overall quirkiness of the form, flash fiction writers may choose a strange POV or outlook on a story.

They might also write from the POV of a narrator who doesn't normally appear in fiction, such as a story told by a cat, a pair of shoes, or a penny lying on the floor of a subway car.

Do It!

These activities support the concepts of this chapter.

Word Count

1.   Write a story of 55 words or fewer (in the tradition of the 55 Fiction Contest).

2.   Write a story that is exactly 100 words long (in the tradition of *http://www.100words.net*).

3.   Write a complete story under 250 words about your life.

Format

1.   Write a story in the form of a suicide note.

2.   Write a story in the form of the Captain's log on a fatal final voyage.

3.   Write a story using dialogue with not only what the characters are saying, but also what they are actually thinking when they say it.

4.   List other unique formats that you might use for a story.

Topic

1. Write a story that contains the words "alabaster" and "vittles."

2. Write a story about a man trying to return a can of tuna to a store clerk who doesn't want to help him.

3. List subjects that are ripe for telling a story.

4. Create several first lines to use in a story.

Weirdness

1. Write a story from the POV of birds watching people while eating at a bird feeder.

2. Write a story from the POV of a cat going to the vet to be "put down" for not using the litter box.

3. Write a story from the POV of a pair of dirty socks.

4. Write a story where everything appears to be normal, but something magical happens and the characters treat it as just an ordinary thing.

First Lines

1. We knew that she was bad the first time she...

2. I really hate to bother you so early in the morning...

3. It all started because of that damn dog...

4. What did he say?

5. When you are pumping gas...

Quick Topics

- Suicide
- Lavender
- Twinkle
- Triangle
- Resume

- Vodka
- Burns
- Dangle
- Lawn mower
- Wrinkle

Chapter 14

Writing the Second Draft

Now that you have got your first draft on the page, you begin the second draft. Your second draft goal is to bring focus and energy to the first draft and begin revising your flash fiction into its final form.

Writing the Second Draft

In order to meet the word constraints of your fiction, you need to find the essence of your story. Now, review your draft carefully and answer these three questions:

1. What happens in the first draft?

The answer to this question is critical. Something has to happen in a story to move it from point A to point B. First drafts may have a lot of good writing in them, but if that good writing doesn't advance the story, you need to get rid of it or save it for another story.

2. Is the focus of the story character, event, or style?

Which focus seems to be the main feature of your draft? Do you have an interesting character or event? Or is this story written in an interesting style that dominates the work? If there doesn't seem to be a clear-cut focus, how would this story work best? What point of view should you use in this story?

One of the biggest problems regarding focus according to Debi Orton, editor of *flashquake* is the: "Failure to maintain clear focus throughout the story, which saps the reader's energy and weakens the narrative drive."

Focus helps anchor the tone and feel of the story.

3. What changes from the beginning to the end?

Some first drafts have little or no change in them at all, so you may have to think about where the change needs to be in this story. If you can't see an obvious change in your story, generate a list of possible changes that might work within it.

Second Draft Writing Guidelines

Look for energy

Good flash fiction radiates energy. When you re-read your story, where do you find the energy? What lines excite you the most? What lines grab your attention? Among these lines, which one anchors the piece? Highlight these lines.

Next, locate the lines that you don't like or drain energy from the piece. Why do these lines make you feel this way? Look for these and highlight them as well.

Can you clearly see the change?

If "a story is a container for change" (*Fast Fiction*), then the change must be easy for the reader to detect. Something has to change between the beginning of the story and the end of it. Read your story and answer the following questions about it:

- Did the situation change?
- Did the character change?
- Did the reader's perception of the character, event, or story change?
- Did you give the reader enough clues to make this believable?

Examples

- Angela, the protagonist in Cathie Byers Hamilton's "Beautiful, Like Gasoline in a Mud Puddle," sees herself as beautiful because of a teacher's praise of her poem.
- In Phoebe Kate Foster's "The Shelf Life of Faceless Dolls and New Men," a man decides to clean up his life after his girlfriend yells at him for being an anal-retentive packrat. He throws out everything, including all of her stuff, to start completely fresh.

Begin in the middle

Flash fiction has to start fast. Begin in the middle of the action, whether it is a fight, a conversation, or a conflict of some sort. The action doesn't need to be dramatic, but this action should lead to the change.

Examples

- Angie DeRosa's "How to Treat a Man" begins in the middle of someone's pounding on an apartment door on a Sunday morning.

- In "Tomato" the story begins in the middle of two-minute date night.

Use surprise

The twist ending is a flash fiction trademark. Not all flash fiction needs a twist, but then again, surprises are always fun.

So throw in a little twist at the end to surprise the reader. Invite the reader in, tell her an interesting story, and just when she thinks she has it figured out, give her an unexpected gift. Make sure that the twist is believable though.

Do It!

These activities support the concepts of this chapter.

1. Take 3 to 5 your first drafts and answer the following questions about them:

    - Did your story have change in it?
    - What was the change?
    - What passages show this change to the reader?

2. Pick your favorite draft from exercise #1 above and rewrite the story focusing on answering these questions, or making the answers clearer to the reader.

3. Begin a story in the middle of:

    - An embarrassing moment
    - A bar brawl
    - Two people having sex
    - An unfair punishment

Writing Exercises

Use these exercises to practice your timed writing skills. Write for 10 minutes about each of the following topics:

1.   A dirty trick

2.   A story containing or about a magical being

3.   A grudge

4.   An unpleasant surprise

5.   A secret found at the bottom of a cedar chest

First Lines

1.   It all started back at the apartment...

2.   What makes you think you're going to get away with...

3.   His worst fear stared him right in the face...

4.   She hated her life and was ready to change it...

5.   You can't go in there...

Quick Topics

- Scrambled eggs
- 8-Ball
- Gravity
- Sock puppet
- Stopping bullets

- Cashews
- Dodgeball
- Gunk
- Fireworks
- Fraud

Chapter 15

Compressing the Narrative for Flash Fiction

Flash fiction has to tell the story of an entire life in a single page. You cannot waste time or words getting to the point so there are several do's and don'ts to follow.

Remember that all rules are meant to be broken, but use these guidelines to help you write your second draft.

Don't

- Write a story that requires a complicated plot.

- Write stories that require a lot of background information or research to help the reader suspend disbelief.

- Select a subject that requires a lot of explanation. Try to break it down into a simpler event. If this doesn't work, maybe this subject's story would be told better using a longer format.

- Have more than three characters. Two seems to be an ideal number for flash fiction.

- Have more than two scenes in a flash fiction story. Keep the number of scenes limited.

- Spend a lot of time creating a complex setting. Set it up as soon as possible — in the first sentence or paragraph.

Do

- Focus on a single event or incident. Look for a moment in time that tells a story.

- Write the story in chronological order by limiting the use of flashbacks or memories to tell the tale. Try to provide background information through dialogue or description.

- Begin in the middle of the event as close to the climax of the story as possible.

- Think of a focus while writing. Are you trying to write about an event, a character, or in a specific tone/point of view, or style?

- Use strong verbs and nouns. Eliminate adjectives and adverbs.

- Remember that "Every word counts double" (from Roberta Allen's *Fast Fiction*).

- Use similes and metaphors to describe and compare different things.

Do It!

Use these exercises to practice your timed writing skills. Write for 10 minutes about each of the following topics:

1. An out-of-control child

2. A dysfunctional family reunion

3. A huge mess

4. Getting someone else in trouble for something you did

5. Getting fired for something stupid

First Lines

1. I can't believe you said that...

2. C'mon, you can trust me...

3. There were three things in the world that she loved...

4. Tell me where it is...

5. He was driving her crazy...

Quick Topics

- Roller coaster
- Gross-out
- Junkyard
- Making waves
- Bad boy

- Gun
- Coral reef
- Teacher's pet
- Miserable
- Weasel

Chapter 16

Revising Flash Fiction

There is no way around it. Flash fiction requires considerable revision. The draft must be pruned, fluffed, cut, weeded, watered, and fed in the correct areas to work. As a flash fiction writer, you will rewrite the piece five, maybe ten times before it can be considered a finished story.

Read work out loud

Reading your work out loud (or better yet, have someone else read your work out loud to you) helps you hear where you need to improve.

If you have someone read it to you, you can hear the awkward pauses, the confusing word choices, and the flaws in the structure. Listening to your words forces you to hear your writing with a different part of your brain. This part doesn't auto-correct a missing modifier or a typo that is not caught by a spell checker (from vs. form, for example).

Reading out loud is the best way to improve your writing. It catches embarrassing mistakes immediately.

Do not edit on-screen

Many people using word processors make edits on the screen. Print out your work and mark it up. Seeing your words on paper helps you make better edits.

Eliminate adjectives and adverbs

Adjectives and adverbs are deadly in flash fiction. They should be eliminated wherever possible. Here are a few of the ways to eliminate them:

- Instead of using adverbs, use strong verbs. Instead of writing "ran quickly" write "sprinted." Instead of writing "spoke quietly" write "whispered."

- Look for words ending in "ly" or "ing"

- Use a good thesaurus to help replace these words.

- Use strong nouns to replace adjectives. Don't write "rusted-out, old car" when "junker" or "jalopy" will do. Use the best noun possible to help the reader visualize your words.

Eliminate empty words

What are empty words? Empty words inflate and slow down flash fiction. They emphasize or modify another word without adding anything vital. Some common empty words are:

- Very
- Really
- More
- Less
- Extremely

Does it feel true?

This one is a little tricky. But think about it. Have you ever read a story, and in the back of your mind you say to yourself, "that's not possible." Or, that's a bit too much to believe.

If you don't quite believe the story when you write it, how do you expect to fool the reader into believing it? It won't happen.

Does this mean that all stories must tell the truth, the whole truth, and nothing but the truth? Absolutely not. It just needs to seem as if it is possible within the context of the story.

If you are writing horror or sci-fi, chances are that you haven't fought off a 700-year-old vampire with a pair of wooden chopsticks and a bulk-size jar of minced garlic. But as the writer you have to make the reader believe that it REALLY happened.

Is it important to the story?

Sometimes a clever line takes away energy from or doesn't advance the story. Remove it or save it for another story.

In flash fiction, there is no room for wasted words. Every single word needs to drive the story to its conclusion. Your story shouldn't have extra sub-plots, characters, or description that don't support this goal. If you are not sure if something is important enough to keep in the story, ask yourself: "Is this word (phrase, sentence, or character) critical to the story?" If your answer is no, eliminate it.

Are you showing or telling?

The hardest thing for any writer to do is to avoid telling the story. If you write that the man was disgusted, this doesn't paint a clear picture for the reader. If you write that the man wrinkled up his nose and turned away as if slapped by the stench, this is a concrete image that the reader can see clearly.

Use metaphor and language to convey images and feelings instead of telling the reader. Let the reader draw her own conclusions.

Eliminate passive voice

This is a plea, to eliminate the dastardly presence of passive voice wherever it can be found. When sentences are written in passive voice, the words can be considered to be watered down or wordy. (Notice the passive voice?)

Active voice uses action. In sentences using active voice, the subject of the sentence acts on the object. In sentences using passive voice, the subject is acted upon by the object. Passive voice usually results in longer sentences, confusing word choices, and awkward phrasing. In other words, passive voice sucks.

Examples

Passive— Seven ferrets are being chased around the living room by my outraged cat.

Active—My outraged cat chased seven ferrets around the living room.

Passive—Chocolate milk has been spilled on mom's new living room carpet.

Active — I spilled chocolate milk on mom's new living room carpet.

Get the opinion of other readers

A writer's best resource is a trusted reader. A good reader gives the writer an honest opinion about the story. This reader tells you what she sees in the work and lets you know what questions she has. A trusted reader acts as a sounding board for your story. This reader doesn't even have to be a writer. Someone who loves to read is perfect for the job.

Limit prepositional phrases

There is little room in flash fiction for prepositional phrases. Try to eliminate as many of them as possible. Specifically, target chains of them linked together.

Examples
- He drove around the block, over the bridge, and through the tunnel.

- He was a man of the cloth.

Less is better

Read through every sentence and see if you can write it using fewer words. Never use six words when three will do. Look for passive voice, empty words, prepositional phrases, adjectives, and adverbs and eliminate them.

Do It!

These activities support the concepts of this chapter.

1.   In one of your drafts, highlight the instances of
      passive voice, empty words, and all adjectives and
      adverbs. Review them carefully. Eliminate as many
      as possible, and re-read the story.

Writing Exercises

Use these exercises to practice your timed writing skills.
Write for 10 minutes about each of the following topics:

1.   A crazy person

2.   A story containing or about an elephant

3.   A nightmare

4.   An evil eye

5.   An immoral science experiment

First Lines

1.   I thought you went to work...

2.   How could you do this to me?

3.   Aha! I knew it all along!

4.   I don't drive because...

5.   You think you have it all figured out...

Quick Topics

- Goddess
- Wednesday
- Body heat
- Two of a kind
- Crash

- Culprit
- Last year
- Summer
- Boils
- Camel

Chapter 17

Marketing Flash Fiction

There are hundreds of markets out there for flash fiction, and many of them are online markets.

Remember: Just because they are online markets doesn't mean you shouldn't take them seriously and follow the same standard rules that you would follow if you were sending a submission to *The New Yorker* or *Ploughshares*.

Guidelines for Submitting Flash Fiction

Study the writers' guidelines

Most online magazines have a guidelines link on the front page. Click it and read it! These writers' guidelines tell you exactly what the editor is and is not looking for. The biggest mistake that new writers make is failing to read and follow the writers' guidelines. According to Mark Budman, editor of *The Vestal Review*, "The problems begin with the submission's formatting — attachments instead of pasted-in text, entries exceeding the word count, poems and essays instead of stories." Reading and heeding the writers' guidelines would prevent these kinds of errors.

Writers' guidelines often are blunt about likes and dislikes. For example:

- No graphic violence or sex please.

- We'd like to see more stories with a humorous "twist" ending.

- We do not accept simultaneous submissions.

- We welcome reprints.

Do not go over the word count limit

This is especially important in flash fiction. If the editor says that the word limit is 1000 words, do not submit a piece that clocks in at 1063 words. It won't even be considered for publication. This doesn't mean that you simply end your story when it reaches the limit. Don't cheat the reader by taking this shortcut.

Edit your work thoroughly

"Inept grammar or poor spelling always leaves a bad impression," says Debi Orton of *flashquake*, "if you can't demonstrate a proficiency with the language, there's no way you can tell a compelling story."

In flash fiction, where every word is critical, you cannot afford a typo or a stupid grammatical error. There is too much competition out there to make these mistakes. Proofread your work and give it to one of your grammar geek friends to look it over as well.

Research your market thoroughly

Read recent issues of the publication you have targeted. What types of stories have they published in the past? Is your story similar? Would your story please the reading audience of this publication?

For example, if your story would clearly be classified as "erotic flash fiction" and the publication that you have targeted has not published anything that could even remotely be classified as erotic, DON'T SUBMIT IT THERE.

Basics of Electronic Submissions

Most online publications do not open attachments to e-mail. With the number of viruses and worms out there, many publications delete e-mail with attachments.

Label your submission clearly

Provide all of the basic information that is needed for your submission. Most publications want the following information:

- Name
- E-mail address
- Mailing address
- Title of your work
- Category in which you are submitting the work (if applicable)
- Phone number

Formatting Electronic Submissions

- Do not use a fancy or unusual font. Stick to Courier, Times New Roman, or Arial.

- If the publication does accept attachments, save the file as an ASCII or Text (.txt) file. Again, check the writers' guidelines to see if the publication accepts attachments.

- Separate paragraphs with a blank line (not an indented tab).

- Copy and paste the story into an e-mail message.

- Make sure that you have the word "SUBMISSION" somewhere in the subject line.

All of these guidelines should be followed unless other specific guidelines are stated in the publication's writers' guidelines. The writers' guidelines are always the final authority on any formatting standards.

Snail Mail Submissions

- Use plain, white 20# paper. Do not use strange colors, onion-skin paper, or fancy card stock.

- Double-space the text of the manuscript. Never submit handwritten work to a publisher.

- Put all essential information on the first page of the work in a standard format

- Use 1" margins around the entire page.

- For submissions that are longer than a page, make sure that a page number, your last name, and a key word are in the header in the upper right-hand corner of the page.

Markets for Flash Fiction

You are now ready to send out your finished, polished stories to markets seeking and publishing flash fiction.

When you're ready to market your flash fiction, a great place to start is subscribing to *Flash Fiction Flash: The Newsletter for Flash Literature Writers*. This is a monthly newsletter edited by Pamelyn Casto, an expert in the field of flash fiction. She has written numerous articles about it and sponsors flash fiction workshops often.

This newsletter features in-depth information about markets that publish flash fiction, prose poetry, flash nonfiction, flash memoirs, and flash plays. Many are paying markets and this newsletter is a fantastic resource if you are out there trying to publish your flash fiction. This magazine also has news of interest to flash literature writers, as well as contest listings and announcements of writers who have successfully published their work. If you are serious about writing flash fiction, this newsletter needs to be arriving in your in-box on a regular basis.

To subscribe, send a completely blank e-mail to FlashFictionFlash-Subscribe@yahoogroups.com

Although many publications, both print and online, publish flash fiction, here are a few of the online markets that seek out and publish flash fiction:

flashquake

flashquake is prestigious online journal for flash fiction, flash nonfiction, and flash poetry. This is a paying market with high standards, very good writers contributing, and excellent writing.

http://www.flashquake.org

The Vestal Review

This is a theme-based electronic market that accepts flash fiction stories under 500 words. The Vestal Review is a quarterly publication. This is an excellent paying market.

http://www.vestalreview.net

55 Fiction Contest

This now-famous contest leads to a lot of great super-short flash fiction. This site has many great examples.

http://www.newtimesslo.com/55_fiction/55_enter.html

Another Realm.com

This is a non-paying science fiction, fantasy, and horror market that takes flash fiction.

http://anotherealm.com/

The First Line

This site publishes flash fiction based on the concept of the given first line. It is a quarterly publication that publishes the best stories that begin with the given first line.

http://www.thefirstline.com/index.htm

Flashshot: Daily Genre Flash Fiction

Non-paying market; recommended for the Bram Stoker Award

FLASHSHOT is a daily dose of genre (Science Fiction, Fantasy, Horror, Mystery, and Surreal) flash fiction usually around 100 words long, sent to your e-mail box every day. All you have to do is subscribe at the e-mail below. It costs you nothing.

http://flashshot.tripod.com/

The Green Tricycle

A fun, very stylish online magazine that specializes in very short flash fiction (under 200 words).

http://greentricycle.com/

Ink Pot/Lit Pot

Ink Pot is the quarterly print journal for Lit Pot Press, which also has an e-zine, *Lit Pot*. Both publish flash fiction. This market also publishes short stories, poetry, and creative nonfiction, features wonderful graphic design, and a pleasing, easy-to-read layout. This is a paying market.

http://www.litpotpress.com/index1.html

PIF Magazine

This is one of the cutting-edge online literary magazines out there. It has been online since 1995 and seems likely to be around for a very long time to come. A good paying online market.

http://www.pifmagazine.com/

ProseAX

This is an award-winning online e-zine that publishes flash fiction.

http://www.proseax.com

Red Writing Hood. com

This site sponsors periodic flash fiction writing contests.

http://redwritinghood.com/

Story House Coffee

Want to have your original work of fiction printed on the label of a can of gourmet coffee? Story House Coffee is your market!

http://www.storyhouse.com/stories/

Toasted Cheese

Nicely-designed, award-winning e-zine that accepts flash fiction (stories under 500 words) and serves as a resource for writers.

http://toasted-cheese.com/index.htm

Would That It Were: The Internet's Premier Magazine of Historical SF

A very specialized science fiction market with a narrow focus, as well as many awards and good pay to back up its high quality.

http://www.wouldthatitwere.com/index.html

Writers' Guidelines Example: flashquake

Below is an example of writers' guidelines from an actual online publication.

> *My comments, indented and in italics like this, follow some of this information.*

EFFECTIVE DECEMBER 1, 2003, WE WILL NO LONGER ACCEPT LAND MAIL SUBMISSIONS

> *Should be a red flag to you. No snail mail submissions will be accepted. Don't waste your stamp!*

These are the guidelines we will use to judge your work.

Ignore them at your peril!

About flashquake

flashquake is an independent, quarterly, web-based publication that focuses on works of flash fiction, flash nonfiction (memoirs, essays, creative nonfiction, humor) and short poetry.

We aim to make flashquake a top quality paying venue for literary writers, and we award stipends to all chosen contributors in each category. We reserve the right to withhold some or all of the stipends to be awarded depending on the quality of the work submitted.

flashquake defines "flash" as fiction and nonfiction of less than 1000 words in length. However, we admire brevity and will receive shorter works favorably. For poetry, our maximum limit is 35 lines per poem. We have no specific guidelines for prose poetry; it must be under our 1000 word limit.

There's your word limit — nothing over 1000 words.

We accept submissions in each of four categories:

- Flash fiction
- Flash nonfiction (memoirs, essays, creative nonfiction, humor)
- Poetry
- Artwork

We're open to any type of writing within those categories, and specifically, we're looking for original work with fresh ideas and strong, clean, concise writing. We will consider reprints of previously published work, as long as the author has retained all rights. We want to see pieces that readers will think about after they've finished reading them.

flashquake seeks the following permissions from its
authors and artists:

- Permission to include your submission in the issue
  of flashquake for which it was submitted, including any future CD and/or audio versions produced;

- Permission to include your submission in
  flashquake's online archives after publication;

- Permission to include your submission in the CD
  version of flashquake awarded to contributors;
  and

- Permission to include your submission in any
  future flashquake CD and/or print anthology.

River Road Studios is the parent company of
flashquake.org and retains the copyright on the publication as a whole (name, design, configuration, etc.). Individual artists retain the rights to their own work.

PUBLICATION SCHEDULE/READING PERIODS

Fall Issue - to be published September 1, 2004 - Our Third
Anniversary Issue

- Submissions accepted June 1 to August 1, 2004

- Contributor Notification Deadline - August 15,
  2004

Winter Issue - to be published December 1, 2004

- Submissions accepted September 1 to November 1,
  2004

- Contributor Notification Deadline - November 15,
  2004

Spring Issue - to be published March 1, 2005

- Submissions accepted December 1, 2004 to February 1, 2005
- Contributor Notification Deadline - February 15, 2005

Summer Issue - to be published June 1, 2005

- Submissions accepted March 1 to May 1, 2005
- Contributor Notification Deadline - May 15, 2005

Any submission received after a deadline has passed will be returned unread.

Pretty straightforward. Here are the deadlines. Heed them!

HOW TO SUBMIT

PROOF YOUR WORK THOROUGHLY! Typographical and grammatical errors distract the reader. Such errors may disqualify your submission, and will certainly make a less than favorable impression on our editors. WE WILL INSTANTLY REJECT ANY SUBMISSION CONTAINING MULTIPLE SPELLING OR GRAMMAR ERRORS.

We do accept simultaneous submissions. Please be sure to tell us immediately if your work is accepted elsewhere.

So sending it several places at once is OK

WE DO NOT ACCEPT MULTIPLE SUBMISSIONS

We do not accept multiple submissions. Submissions are restricted to one piece of work per author/artist in any single category per reading period. This means that one writer could send us one short story, one memoir and one poem in the same reading period, and that we would consider all three pieces. However, if one writer sent us two short stories, we would only accept the first one received.

> *So don't insult the editors by sending more than one story in the same category in that reading period.*

Further, if your submission is rejected, you may not resubmit it, or any other work in that same category until the next reading period.

E-MAIL SUBMISSIONS:

If you are new to electronic submissions, please read our Notes on Preparing Your Work.

Make sure that you include the following information in your submission:

- Name
- E-mail address
- Address
- Title of your work
- The category in which you are submitting
- A short (no more than 100 words) biography written in third person
- Whether the piece has been previously published and if so, where

> *To show the editor that you are a true professional, you should do this without fail.*

Paste your submission into a PLAIN TEXT e-mail message addressed to submit@flashquake.org.

WE WILL NOT OPEN ATTACHMENTS TO E-MAIL!

> *So HTML messages are out, and don't bother attaching a file to the e-mail.*

Label your message with the category in which your submitting and the title of your work (e.g., Fiction Submission: My Story Title).

Be sure to use a standard font, such as Courier. Separate your paragraphs with a blank line.

Check and double-check your message before hitting the Send key.

Tells you exactly how the editors expect to receive a submission. Don't use tabs or fancy, weird fonts.

SUBMISSION NOTIFICATION

Writers submitting work for publication will be notified via e-mail about the status of their submissions within one week of the publication date, or sooner if possible.

We provide feedback from our reviewers (comments from 2-6 editors) about work considered so that writers will know why we've accepted or rejected a particular piece. These are not in-depth critiques, but subjective comments from our editors and may not be positive in nature. The comments returned from our editors are unvarnished and have offended some who receive them.

Reviewers' comments about the work will automatically be forwarded along with your notification. The majority of feedback we've received about supplying our editors' comments has been overwhelmingly positive. However, if you are apprehensive about receiving honest comments about your work, please indicate on your submission that you would prefer not to see the comments.

Wow! They take your work very seriously! Blunt honesty! Refreshing. Don't bother following up to see if the story has been accepted until the week before the publication date. If the date goes by and you still haven't heard anything, then follow up.

PAYMENT OF STIPENDS

Submissions in each writing category will be judged by our editors, whose decisions are final. All published authors will receive payments ranging from $5 - $25, which will accompany the contributor's CD copy of the issue, within two weeks of publication (delivery to non-U.S. contributors may require longer than two weeks). The actual amount to be paid will be decided by our editors' ranking of the work. All authors and artists whose work is accepted for publication will receive a CD version of the issue in which their work was published.

Here is the payment rate information! You don't need to ask about it, it is spelled out for you!

Do It!

These activities support the concepts of this chapter.

1. Review some of the example markets mentioned in this chapter. Print the writers' guidelines for each of them. Do any of your stories fit these requirements?

2. Sign up for Pamelyn Casto's *Flash Fiction Flash: The Newsletter for Flash Literature Writers*.

Writing Exercises

Use these exercises to practice your timed writing skills. Write for 10 minutes about each of the following topics:

1. Someone who worries too much

2. Two people who can't stand each other trapped together

3. A knife in the back

4. An animal with special powers

5.   A deadly competition

First Lines

1.   I dreamt of freedom...

2.   Don't run...

3.   All heads in the room turned toward her/him...

4.   It was a catastrophe...

5.   Who was that?

Quick Topics

- Chopping
- Idiot
- Treasure
- Bulls eye
- Nerves

- Hunter
- Warm milk
- God fearing
- Oven
- Lincoln

Chapter 18

Where to Go From Here

OK. Now that you know the flash fiction writing technique, have written a few stories, and have just about finished this book, you may be asking yourself: What do I do now? Where do I go from here?

Practice, practice, practice

Writing a few stories is never enough. You must keep practicing every day. Set aside a little bit of time, 15 to 30 minutes, and continue writing using flash fiction writing topics, or those you come up with on your own.

Take additional classes or join a writers' group

Taking a writing class or joining a writers' group is an important step for all writers. Building a network, and getting your work looked at and critiqued by other writers, is essential if you hope to be published.

Look for markets for your work

Send out your finished, polished stories to markets that are seeking and publishing flash fiction. This keeps your writing skills sharp, and encourages you to read the publications you hope will publish your work.

Don't give up

The writers who succeed are the writers who keep writing despite the distractions, the long hours, the loneliness, and the numerous rejection slips. These writers study their craft and constantly challenge themselves to improve their work. They take writing classes, participate in writers' groups and attend writers' conferences. They write because they love to do it, and with a lot of skill and a little luck, they just might make a little money.

Do It!

Use these exercises to practice your timed writing skills. Write for 10 minutes about each of the following topics:

1. A gut feeling

2. Someone doing something against his/her will

3. The monster that lives under your bed.

4. A frightening day at the zoo.

5. Forgetting something very important

First Lines

1. I can't remember...

2. Nathan and Bertha were the perfect couple...

3. I could tell by the look in her eyes that...

4. Mom, I don't want you to get upset, but...

5. The knife sank deep into his flesh...

Quick Topics

- Cheesy
- Invisible
- Superhero
- Stooge
- Bowel movement

- Mary
- Witchcraft
- You are here
- Roof
- Widow

Appendix A

Story Examples

The Escape of The Circus Freaks
by Bruce Boston

The escape of the circus freaks was nothing to laugh about.

Some of them were harmless enough: the bearded lady, the man with the ears and hooves of a goat, the woman with the body of a Rubens and the head of a catfish, scales and tentacle-whiskers and walleyed vision to match.

Yet there were others who posed a serious threat to public sanity.

What if the Mesmer Man invaded the privacy of your bedroom while you were helplessly lost in bland blue slumber? He could forge any illusion he chose in the chambers of your unconscious: orange waves, yellow skies, emerald peninsulas piercing your brain with forests fiendishly quixotic in the fauna and flora they had to offer.

What if the Knife Boy arrived at a shopping mall or a major thoroughfare during the Christmas rush, hurling his ready stream of acid jibes and razor-sharp edges at hapless pedestrian shoppers, cutting to the quick of the bright commercial spirit, leaving holiday blood slathered in smears and droplets on kiosks and plate glass windows?

Imagine the quarantines required and man-hours lost if the Siamese Quintuplets exposed their lascivious dance and outlandish ways to the eager glance of an ingenue generation. Picture your children with their eyes bulging out of their heads and the veins throbbing in their temples.

Think of them all, freaks in concert, rampaging through the failing light of a dusk we could not control, peering in our windows, running in and out of the shadows, pounding on our doors with hands that had no doubt fondled their own distorted bodies and one another's in obscene detail.

And then the night burning with new phantoms we had yet to fathom.

And what of the potential for bicameral chaos and the legislative stampedes this would inevitably entail? Remember that hysteria and trampled death are not uncommon in partisan relations.

This could have been a case brandished in media sensation for federal scrutiny and a score of ad hoc committees. Yet it was swiftly squelched in vast favor of events more suited to the masses, whose hungers can be ravenous and far from refined.

Let us be thankful the trusty Circus Police, diminutive yet energetic, twelve to a car and forever inventive in their slapstick antics, managed to corral this ragged cast of dangerous miscreants before harm could be delivered to the equipoise of our palatable metropolis and axiomatic nation.

Let us pass the buttered popcorn and pay homage to the carnival gods who have placed these entertaining yet vigilant guardian-clowns at our imminent disposal.
(425 words)

Originally published in the October 2003 issue (#15) of *The Vestal Review*

How to Treat a Man

by Angie DeRosa

The first time I betrayed a friend, I told Sasha that I had no idea where her boyfriend might be. She came over on a Sunday morning, running up to the door of my apartment, pounding, pounding, pounding, then ringing the doorbell over and over again, as if her finger was permanently stuck in the doorbell hole. I knew it was her. She called three times that morning, and it wasn't even 10 a.m. I stood behind the door, watching her pace back and forth, then stare into the peephole. I watched her pull up her sunglasses to hold back her long, straight blonde hair. I watched her put her hands on her hips, pace back and forth again, out of the range of the peephole, then back into my range. I tiptoed from the door, down my hallway on the pergo floor, and I ran, all the way to the door, swinging it open. It was all about the delivery.

"I haven't heard from Mick," she said, keeping the door open with her right foot and using her hip to force her way past me into the entryway. I slipped on my flipflops, and went out onto the porch. She followed, thank goodness, and sat next to me on the stairs.

"Did he call you last night?" I asked.

"No," she said, picking a tulip out of my flower garden. "I don't know what to think about him anymore. We've only been dating for a few months, but it seemed like things were going fine."

I kept looking back at the door, hopeful that she wouldn't be able to sense his presence. I told him to stay in the bedroom. I hope he'd listen. He couldn't be that stupid. Did I smell like him? I lowered my head to my chest, stretching my arms out in front of me in order to get a whiff. Mick and I just hit it off. It was instant chemistry, when two people can't take their eyes off each other. Sasha wasn't good to him anyway. I watched them interact at the bar on Friday night. Then, his eye would catch my eye and I'd have a mouthful of ice that I'd keep in my right cheek, and I'd move the ice around, and release it back into the glass, and run my tongue over my lips. I had to give him something else to think about, something other than Sasha's visit to the gynecologist.

She didn't know how to treat a man. She completely overlooked his sensitivities and needs and why shouldn't he come running to my arms?

"You're not listening to me," Sasha said, standing up in a huff, and throwing the tulip into the grass. "I'm trying to tell you how worried I am about my relationship with Mick, and you're off in la-la land somewhere, and you didn't even bother to answer my calls this morning."

Then, she punched me twice in the arm with her bony little fist. She tore a second tulip from the ground, whacked me on the head with the root end of it, and stomped off down the driveway. See, I told you she doesn't know how to treat a man. **(537 words)**

The Shelf Life of Faceless Dolls and New Men
by Phoebe Kate Foster

It all began with rogue condiments.

When she opened a cabinet, the packets of catsup, mustard and soy sauce you'd saved from years of takeout orders threw themselves at her. "You're a pathological packrat!" she snapped. "As if that's not irritating enough, you buy stuff and never use it!" She pointed at pantry shelves. "What a waste!" She checked the labels on the interesting things you'd found at the supermarket instead of the humdrum items on her list.

"Past their expiration dates," she announced, and threw out your maraschino cherries, mock turtle soup, mushroom powder, marshmallow fluff, jalapeño dip, tamarind paste, lichee nuts and snack cakes.

"How can a jar of cocktail onions get old?" you asked, as she tossed those, too.

"Nothing lasts forever." She gestured at the rooms beyond. "Just look around! Your old junk is everywhere. You've never thrown out anything in your life. Believe me, you'd feel like a new man if you did."

After she left for work, muttering about anal-retentive people, you decided she was right.

Into trash bags you shoved your badminton equipment, backgammon set, ab wheel, stamp collection, Popular Mechanics issues, baseball cards, action figures, souvenirs from Disneyland and Graceland, Beatles posters, acoustic guitar, collegiate sweatshirts, clothes in sizes you'd never fit again, presents of apparel you said you liked, old letters, photo albums with faces you preferred to forget, address books full of people you didn't actually like, and Mont Blanc fountain pen stand, a gift from her. The intended dig was inescapable, in light of the debacle of your so-called career.

You suddenly realized there were many things you'd wanted to throw out for a long time: pottery lamps, Picasso prints, coffee table books, crystal figurines, that collection of faceless dolls -- they gave you the creeps -- and vases of peacock feathers. The thought of bare-butted birds deprived of both plumage and pride depressed you.

Finally, in the bedroom, you emptied a bureau, closet and nightstand, and hauled everything out to the curb for the garbage truck.

It was done. And it felt good.

At dusk, you stand at the window, waiting. A taxicab pulls up and she gets out. She stares, slack-mouthed, at the black Hefties lining the street like body bags after a bad accident. The wind catches a white silk chemise and waltzes it away with the debris in the gutter. Dazed, she circles the garbage, rescuing random items -- a doll, a book, a necklace, a feather -- and clutches them to her, as if to staunch a wound.

A dismal drizzle leaks from the darkening sky. Her eyes seek out the apartment window on the second floor. Her upturned face is wet. With rain or tears? You aren't sure. She raises her arms to you. In accusation? Supplication? You shrug, draw the curtains and pour a celebratory Scotch.

Naturally, she's upset, but you know she understands. After all, she'd be the first to say never keep anything beyond its shelf life. **(497 words)**

Originally published in the October 2003 issue (#15) of *The Vestal Review*

Beautiful, Like Gasoline in a Mud Puddle
by Cathie Byers Hamilton

Daddy walloped Crystal this morning. She'd spilled the last of the milk all over the floor, and there was nothing for him to put on his cereal. He smacked her upside the head and yelled, "Shit, Crystal, watch what you're doing! That damn milk is expensive!" Mama wasn't home, so the milk never did get mopped up.

I'm eleven years old and Crystal is seven. I'm in the fifth grade at South Chesterfield Elementary, and Crystal's in the first. Crystal should be in the second grade, but she had to repeat kindergarten; she's had a hard time remembering all of her letters. I tried to help her a little, but she didn't get it. Crystal's not one for learning. She told me that those letters swam in front of her, like teeny tadpoles in a jar. She told me that all of those letters looked exactly the same.

I've always been good at school. One day when I was in second grade, I overheard my teacher, Mrs. Kuhn, tell the guidance counselor that I had a "knack for language arts," which was apparently surprising to her, "considering the girl's home life." At the time, I didn't quite understand what that meant, so I asked Mama about it. Mama told me that she didn't understand it, either. She told me that those "damn teachers don't know what they're talking about half the time, anyway." Mama never went to another parent-teacher conference after that.

Because of Crystal spilling the milk, it took us a little longer than usual to get ready for school. Crystal cried after Daddy hit her. She decided that she was "very sick" and told me that she did not feel like going to school. Crystal likes to stay home with Daddy, but I don't. I go to school, even if I have a sore throat. I go to school, even when I've just thrown up and my whole body aches. There are no beds to rest in at my house, except Daddy's. There's no time to rest, either. When you stay home from school, Daddy expects you to make him lunch and keep him company.

We'd learned to write limericks in language arts last week, and today, we were going to write haikus. I was very excited because Mr. Clark sometimes picked the best poem and read it to the class. He'd read Jessica's on Friday. None of my stuff had been read, yet, but I kept my fingers crossed. Today could be that special day.

I got to school late. Mrs. Byron, the attendance monitor, screamed at me in the back hallway as she wrote my late pass, her letters like Daddy-Long Legs on the page. She leaned toward me and whispered as I walked past her, "Take a bath before you come to school tomorrow, Angela. Water's free." When I got to Mr. Clark's room, the class had already started doing their morning work.

"Haikus are a very structured form of poetry," Mr. Clark told us, "Five syllables, seven syllables, then, five syllables."

5, 7, 5, I repeated to myself. 5, 7, 5.

I hunched over my desk, imagining a garden, full of color. I imagined little creatures - frogs, crickets, and inchworms - busying themselves. I pictured a place

where the rain splattered against leaves, where everything was rich and green and full of life.

Bright butterflies sail

Across morning so quiet

Noisy solitude.

"Angela, is your head itchy?" I was so busy writing that I
almost didn't realize that Mr. Clark was talking to me.

I hadn't thought about it much, but yeah, my head was
itchy. I scratched it again as I answered him.

"Angela, I think you need to go have the nurse take a
look at your head."

I'd been through this drill before, a million times. I
glanced at my poem one last time as I pushed my chair
back and stood up. The other kids snickered. They knew
where I was going. Jessica Jones leaned towards the coat
rack, away from me, as I walked past her desk.

Miss Tanya ran a comb through my hair. It tickled. Lice,
she pronounced immediately. Miss Tanya didn't even
ask me for my parents' phone number so that she could
call them and let them know that they needed to pick me
up. She knew that we didn't have a phone. She went to
the coat rack and grabbed her jacket. "C'mon, Angela,"
she sighed, "Let's get you home."

Miss Tanya let me go back to the classroom to get my
coat and my book bag. I shuffled slowly down the hall. I
knew that once I arrived at the room, the kids would all
laugh about my "cooties." I also knew that Daddy
wouldn't mess with my hair today, and Mama would be
too tired after work to shampoo it for me. Tomorrow, I
would be as welcome in school as a cockroach on a
cookie.

Mr. Clark helped me get my things together. He gave me
a geometry worksheet to complete for homework. He
was holding my poem, but he didn't hand it to me.

"Angela, your poem is beautiful. If it's okay with you, I'd like to read it to the class this afternoon."

Even though my head was so itchy, I didn't scratch it. Even though I felt sick about going home, I forgot about Daddy. For one second, I got down in Mr. Clark's words. I lived in my poem. My poem was "beautiful."

If my words could be beautiful, then I could be, too.
(926 words)

Originally published in the Winter 2003/2004 issue of *flashquake*

Ice Cream
by M. K. Hobson

She is too big for her apartment.

Six feet tall, she is always breaking things and bruising herself and ducking involuntarily. Japan, land of the small. Small island, small people, small apartments, small bathrooms. Her bathroom is four feet square, to be precise. She sits in the tepid bathtub, knees to chin. The tub is deeper than it is wide; it's like bathing in a drinking glass.

"Tonight I will be at Brendan's," she thinks, closing her eyes. "He will get me ice cream." The thought is almost unbearably pleasant.

She meets Brendan at a stand bar that's the size of a Greyhound bus-station bathroom. She sits hunched over a plate-sized table to keep from knocking her head on a low-hanging Styrofoam lobster. Brendan is Welsh. He has a large head and a beaky nose, and he talks about football. She knows nothing about football. She lets him talk for the requisite hour, nodding. Then she touches his thigh with her knee and says the same thing she always does:

"Let's go to your place."

It's a beautiful warm night, low and purple. She leads the way, like a dog pulling at a leash. He chuckles at her back.

"You're always so eager," he says, and pride at his assumed prowess brightens his tone. He doesn't understand. He wouldn't be flattered if he did.

Brendan's apartment is on the top floor of a pre-war building built of red cedar and white pine. She squeezes past him, running up the narrow stairs, waiting for him on the landing, wiggling with anticipation. He unlocks the door and she kicks off her shoes. She hurries down the wood-panelled hall and slides the shoji screen to one side.

Six tatamis glow up at her. Twelve feet by nine feet of gleaming space, devoid of furniture, empty. The beauty of it makes her stomach twist.

She stretches herself out on the gleaming floor, extending her feet and hands as far as they can go. She closes her eyes and smooths the backs of her arms against the slippery woven grass.

Brendan stands in the doorway, looking down at her. He half-smiles as he unbuttons his shirt. The profundity of impending loss electrifies her.

"Ice cream," she says.

He frowns.

"Again?"

"It's a warm night, wouldn't it be nice?"

He rolls his eyes, but he buttons his shirt back up.

She hears the clutter of keys and the shuffle of heavy feet down wooden steps. She closes her eyes. She breathes, in and out. It is a delicious effort, moving air through the great space around her.

In ten minutes he's back. A pint of green tea ice cream bulges in a white plastic bag.

"Hard as a rock," he said huskily, pleadingly. "Needs time to sit."

She sighs. Fair is fair. She opens her arms to him. Holds her breath.

"Let it sit, then," she says.

Grinning, he lowers himself over her, encloses her, enfolds her.

And again, the world is small. **(497 words)**

Originally published in the October 2003 issue (#15) of *The Vestal Review*

The Dead
by Beverly Jackson

We walk every morning, our pace well suited-old dog and old woman-a leash uniting us in silent journeys down country roads. The Redwoods and Douglas firs creak in winter gusts that push us along. The sky is a changing panorama of purest pinks and the clear blues of newborns' eyes. Glorious enough to explain why people think heaven is skyward. The mist steams on a horizon of pines.

A dead mouse in the road is tiny, scrawny, with gray fur. If not for the black ooze beneath its head, it looks asleep. I drag Murphy away, his nose urged toward the scent.

The following morning, we see a thin snake flattened on the pavement, its scales glittery in the early light. Its skin is unharmed, like a flower pressed under the wheels of a car or truck. As I again yank Murphy from the kill, I see movement-an infant is silhouetted, perched high in a tall, soft fir. It's a flash, an image. I cup my hand over my eyes, but she is gone-a mirage.

Next outing, bitter cold, the trudge up Arcadia Road is arduous. Murphy's fur ripples against his flanks in the wind. I wonder, for the millionth time, how different life might be, had the child been born. I shiver with cold and my dark thoughts.

"Better take a quick whiz, Murph," I say. The wind shakes the trees, making a whooshing eerie rustle. The dawn skies are flat and gray.

On the road an injured wren huddles, motionless. I hold Murphy back as I swoop it up. It struggles only a little. I move it gently to the grassy shoulder where it sits, immobile, while my mind battles between leaving it to survive in nature, or taking it home. Murphy's interest has been captured by a movement in the trees.

The baby appears again in the fir. No mistake. She is perched naked and rosy on an outer limb. The tight curls of her hair are honey-colored, and her face dimples with mirth as she waves her tiny fist.

It begins in my chest, and explodes in my ears, filling my mouth and nose. My head rings with the screech of wind and cries that must be born in my own constricted throat.

For years I've wondered what she'd look like, this child of mine. She gaily waves and I lift my hand in response, as if our fluttering fingers spin a thread, forever connecting us. She waits, I now know.

The vision of her fades in and out of the dappled foliage of the woods.

At my feet, the bird takes a few faltering steps, and I swipe my wet face with the sleeve of my parka. When I look back, the empty branches, heavy with needles, sway, waving.

The wren lifts off in a dazed and haphazard little circle. Then, buoyed by wind, it soars up into the trees.
(489 words)

Originally published in the December 2003 issue (#16) of *The Vestal Review*

Mr. Potato In My Head
by Derrick Lin

When I was younger, my mother explained to me that I had a dirty potato in my head. She tilted my head on her lap, took a cotton swabbed Q-tip and gently prodded and probed, cleaning out the earwax as I held my breath in fear. "If you don't clean out your ears once in a while, the potato will push out your brain," she said. When she was done poking at my ear, she held the swab out for me to see. "Look," she said, "Lots of potato." I admired the dirty golden wax on the end of her swab and wondered how I got a potato in my ear and how big it could possibly grow.

It was disturbing to think that all I was learning at school could be rendered meaningless by the sprouting of a tuber. I pictured a starchy, stony potato slowly expanding and squeezing out the soft spaghetti-like brain until nothing remained but icky stringy goo and the remnants of me dumb as a log. My great obsession in life became the excavation of that potato. As I watched TV, as I studied for my spelling tests, as I picked carrots off my plate at the dinner table, my finger was in my ear scraping away as much potato as I could. (Nothing but my finger though because there was a little drum in my ear that I didn't want to damage.) No matter how much potato I removed, sooner or later there was always more.

Too late, my mom tried to bring an end to my fixation. She decided to level with me, explaining that she had been joking about the potato. The flaky gold I mined was a waxy discharge produced by glands in the ear to protect the delicate instruments inside from dust and other particles. (There must be a whole band, not just a drum.) On some level what she said made sense. I finally understood why the potato flakes from my ear tasted acrid and not like my French fries or potato chips. Still, knowing it was wax instead of potato failed to mitigate my behavior. Instead of dirty vegetable, I pictured dirty crayon, but it was still something that didn't belong in my head, pressuring my tender mind.

My mother's biology lessons and admonishments were only partially successful. I stopped picking my ears in her presence or anyone else's. Instead I waited until I was alone, and in private shame I continued to poke at my ears. I knew that what I was doing was wrong, but I could not stop touching them. The delicate nerve endings in my ear let me know that I was alive. Then, I would look at the tip of my finger for the little bits of waxy something coming from me. It was all so maddeningly sensual.

I began collecting the granules of earwax in a Ziploc sandwich bag hidden in the bottom of my sock drawer. Eventually, I had enough wax to pack together into a lump the size of a real potato. Finally, I could visualize the thing growing inside my head. I would roll it in my hands, slowly adding to it, marveling as it grew and grew.

Eventually, the small potato became a very large potato. I cleared a spaced at the back of my closet for when my earwax potato would be as large as my head. But my mom must have found it while folding my laundry. One day I found my clear plastic bag empty and in the waste of the bathroom. She must have known what it was, and that I would find out, but she too embarrassed to confront me. She never spoke of it. Still, I did not stop, and she pretended she did not know.

I continued until one day there was a small ache at the base of my skull. Anytime I felt any sort of physical discomfort, I associated it with the potato crushing my brain, killing me slowly. There was the unpleasant sensation of something tugging at my ears. My ears felt uncomfortably full, and I wanted to dig, but my ears were sensitive and ached to touch. As my hearing slowly faded, my head throbbed painfully. I lay in bed, eyes closed, waiting for the potato to sprout from my head. I hoped that it would sprout from somewhere in the back of my head, where it could be covered by my hair. Though I feared that it would sprout from the spot right between my eyes.

Gradually the pain worsened. I could feel the potato crushing my brain to the side of my skull. The pressure built slowly. Every time I blinked, I thought my head was going to explode. If I were going to suffer the ignominy of death by potato I wished it could at least end quicker.

Eventually, I tried to get up and seek help. I stood, but only for an instant as the world spun and the floor rose up to greet my face. Bam! I tried to push myself away from the suddenly gravity defying floor, but with a deft spin it struck me again. Bam!

My mom found me semi-conscious on the floor and took me to the hospital. It turned out that I had otitis media otherwise known as an ear infection. Although the doctor said my illness had nothing to do with potatoes or my constant ear picking he told me I should keep my finger out of my ear.

Every day I battle the urge to pick. There is no twelve-step program to cure my suffering, just me and a cold dead turkey in the back of my freezer that I talk to once in a while. **(961 words)**

Originally published in the Winter 2003/2004 issue of *flashquake*

Tomato

by Clint Meadows

It's Two-Minute Date night at this bar you hate, where you're shoved with someone of the opposite sex for two minutes and then forced to move on. The idea is that if one of your two-minute prospects seems to be worthwhile, you get their name and number before time is up and then you call them later.

Your dead father is laughing.

There are televisions in every dark corner of the bar, hanging from the walls and ceiling like radioactive cobwebs.

You want to tell her why you hate this bar so much, but you don't have time.

On television is a rerun of Cheers.

"My father," you tell the flat-faced girl who is your current girlfriend, "he used to be a professional laugh track recorder. He had this amazing laugh."

You want to describe his laughter to her, but you don't have time.

The girl looks at you with lifeless eyes.

"He was a laugher for Cheers," you clarify, pointing up at the television.

"Really," the girl says, gnawing on the straw of her bloody mary and looking past you, at somebody else who isn't you. Her flat, skinny body is trapped tightly in this long pink sequined dress that makes her look like cow tongue.

You try to think of a compliment for this dress, a nicer description, but you don't have time.

"Yeah," you say. "But that was just something he did in his free time. He was otherwise a novelist."

"A what?"

"A novelist. He wrote big long books about places and people."

The girl jiggles her bony arm and then looks down at her twine-sized wristwatch. "I'd rather be a laugher."

"That's funny," you say, and the girl looks at you blankly.

You say tomato and she says tomato.

"Does he still laugh?" She asks.

"No, he's dead now."

"How'd he die?" she says.

You take a swig of your beer and shake your head. You notice she has a scar on her face - your mind whirls between possible causes - but before you can ask her about it, the bell rings and she moves on to her next boyfriend.

Above you, your dead father is laughing. **(361 words)**

Originally published in the Winter 2003/2004 issue of *flashquake*

The Moon Complements My Shadow

by Margaret B. Simon

Sometimes in your secret dreams you carve a hole inside yourself and wait for someone to come along and fill it. And some do come along who almost fit, but not quite. Others come to you as fog who try to fill and fit everything. I explained this once to my shrink. When he moved to Manhattan, I stopped trying to explain anything.

Forget that hole inside. Life is too short. "Make no entangling alliances," was my father's motto, and he was right. But wrong about me not being able to make a living as a writer. Still, a man has certain needs. I forget about the dreams, plug the hole with one hooker after another, strung out from here to Jupiter and back again. A crash for cash. Some last long enough to turn me on. One or two enjoy it. I forget their faces more quickly than their names.

The skinny one with the knapsack catches my eye. She waves to me, so I pull over, let the window down far enough to hear her price, but she won't say. Gives me some story about her car I don't need to know. Wants me to take her to the Greyhound Station. Sure, right. But I go along with it, tell her I'll be glad to do this tomorrow morning, but that I'm going home and would she like to have a good night's sleep or is she in too much of a hurry. I can't believe she doesn't seem to catch the sarcasm.

In my apartment, she stops to look at the bookshelf. Squats, pulls one volume out and reads a phrase aloud. She asks me questions about the author. "It's a pen name," I tell her. Probably say more than I mean to.

I offer her a drink but she says she'd rather have coffee, if that's okay. So I find myself in my kitchen instead of my bedroom. She finds some crackers and a jar of peanut butter, keeping up a steady stream of conversation while she eats, the kind of conversation you could have with anyone if you knew them well enough. Somewhere along in there, between the smiles and silly jokes, I begin to realize that she's for real.

The evening becomes a passage. Somehow none of it surprises me. Like when we wind up listening to Cusco's latest CD, or when I find myself telling her things I never told that effing shrink. I watch in her eyes and listen to her voice. I notice the way she holds her coffee mug close to her mouth and how when she takes a sip her upper teeth show.

So midnight comes and goes. It might have lasted longer, that night. I don't know, never will. I decide I won't be taking her to the bus station. She's just too close. She should be fog.

I pretend that she has a book I wrote in her knapsack. Not my usual, something different. She falls asleep on the couch and I cover her with a blanket before I turn in.

When morning comes I put her in a cab, and like a dude cowboy slap the trunk as it takes off. So she leaves quietly with her knapsack and her straggly blonde hair, which I noticed was dark at the roots. I try to forget her eyes, a silvery blue with indigo coronas. I try to forget the light from those eyes. But she has my phone number and my address in her pocket.

Two weeks late she writes she's got a job waiting tables in a cafe somewhere in Kansas. Calls me sometimes on Sundays, says how the food is rewardingly greasy and makes jokes about the people she meets. She seems happy, and this is good. Says she's almost saved enough for a PC.

I finish my next novel: Sex Slaves of the Orient. Another sure thing I can bet on, pay debts with, play with, carry on my lifestyle with, take to my grave.

Think I'll send her a check so she can get the damned computer early. Maybe she'll make it on her own. She's safe there, far away from me. She didn't have my book in her knapsack. She had a manuscript. It wasn't bad, but it wasn't porn or anything else you could sell.

Tonight I walk home alone, pleased with the way the moon complements my shadow, makes me tall.
(741 words)

Originally published in the Fall 2003 issue of *flashquake*

I Hope He Likes It

by Charles Tuomi

I hope he likes it.

I hope it works.

But if he finds something wrong with it? If he shakes that big head in disapproval, or runs one beefy index finger - tsk, tsk, tsk - over the other...?

I don't even want to think about it.

He won't let me stay here if he doesn't like it.

I hear him now, like a thunderstorm a few miles off: That booming voice cracking jokes, and other people guffawing along with him, as they always do, obediently.

He's headed this way.

I don't see him, not yet, but I know what he'll look like, what he always looks like. Nothing about him ever changes. He'll have a pasty soft suburban face, but his uniform will be dark, and as sharp as the blade on a city kid's knife. You could lose a finger running it over the crease in his pants. You could lose the contents of your bladder looking into his deep-set eyes.

You could lose everything, just by pissing him off. Trust me on that.

I take it out again, turn it over in my hands. It looks good, feels fine, I guess. No obvious imperfections, nothing I can detect but then, who am I, and what do I know about these things? I don't even know the name of the woman I bought it from.

He's the expert. He's the one who knows.

And he's so close now, just a few feet away, god he's fast. As I sink lower in my seat, pressing my knees against the cushion in front of me, I glimpse the dark black tip of his hat. The thought of hiding occurs, hiding or fleeing, but it's too late for either.

He thanks someone, thanks someone else - god he's polite, he hides that malice so well - thanks a heavy woman in a tank top two seats up. He says something clever, to which someone else chuckles. Across the aisle from me, a balding man in a business suit smiles, too.

I should force a smile. That would be good, but the muscles on my face refuse. My bladder feels full. It's almost my turn. One more row of seats and he'll be here, practically on top of me, scrutinizing, dark eyes probing, for what I don't, I really don't, know. I never know what he's looking for, what he's really looking for...

He takes his eyes from the woman in the seat in front of me and drops them right. on. me. He presses a small plastic counting device in his left hand - click - and smiles plasticly, raises his thick eyebrows beneath a dark blue cap like a pilot's, and nods. It's my turn.

"Ticket, please," he says.

My hand shakes as I go for my wallet, where the little blue stub is. I've never used this one before. I just bought it at the station before I got on the train.

I hope it works.

I hope he likes it. **(496 words)**

Originally published in the Fall 2003 issue of *flashquake*

Appendix B

Suggested Reading

Story Collections

Flash Fiction: 72 Very Short Stories, eds. James Thomas, Denise Thomas, Tom Hazuka. W.W. Norton, 1992.

Micro Fiction: An Anthology of Really Short Stories, ed. Jerome Stern. W.W. Norton, 1996.

Short Shorts: An Anthology of the Shortest Stories, eds. Irving Howe and Ilana Wiener Howe. Bantam, 1999.

Sudden Fiction, ed. James Thomas and Robert Shapard. Gibbs Smith Publisher, 1987.

Sudden Fiction (Continued): 60 New Short Stories, eds. James Thomas and Robert Shapard. W.W. Norton, 1996.

Sudden Fiction International: Sixty Short-Short Stories, eds. James Thomas and Robert Shapard. W.W. Norton, 1989.

The World's Shortest Stories: Murder, Love, Horror, Suspense, All This and Much More in the Most Amazing Short Stories Ever Written, Each One Just 55 Words Long, ed. Steve Moss. Running Press Book Publishers, 1998.

Myths, Fables, Fairy Tales

The Complete Fairy Tales of the Brothers Grimm, Translated by Jack Zipes; Bantam, 1987.

Mythology, Edith Hamilton. Back Bay Books, 1998.

Urban Legends

The Baby Train & Other Lusty Urban Legends, Jan Harold Brunvand. W.W. Norton, 1993.

Writing: Exercises and Prompts

The Pocket Muse: Ideas and Inspirations for Writing, Monica Wood. Writer's Digest Books, 2002.

Story Starters, Lou Willett Stanek. Avon Books, 1998.

What If? Writing Exercises for Fiction Writers, Anne Bernays and Pamela Painter. HarperCollins, 1995.

The Writer's Block: 786 Ideas to Jump-Start Your Imagination, Jason Rekulak. Running Press, 2001.

Writing Fiction

Fast Fiction: Creating Fiction in Five Minutes, Roberta Allen. Story Press, 1997.

Fiction Writer's Workshop, Josip Novakovich. Story Press, 1995.

If You Can Talk, You Can Write, Joel Saltzman. Warner Books, 1993.

Immediate Fiction, Jerry Cleaver. St. Martin's Press, 2002.

The Plot Thickens: 8 Ways to Bring Fiction to Life, Noah Lukeman. St. Martins Press, 2001.

Stein on Writing, Sol Stein. St. Martin's Griffin, 1995.

The Writer's Idea Book, Jack Heffron. Writer's Digest Books, 2000.

The Writer's Idea Workshop: How to Make Your Good Ideas Great, Jack Heffron. Writer's Digest Books, 2003.

Writing Fiction Step by Step, Josip Novakovich. Story Press, 1998.

The Writing Life

Bird by Bird: Some Instructions on Writing and Life, Anne Lamott. Anchor, 1995.

Escaping Into the Open: The Art of Writing True, Elizabeth Berg. HarperCollins, 1999.

On Writing: A Memoir of the Craft, Stephen King. Scribner, 2000.

poemcrazy: Freeing Your Life with Words, Susan Goldsmith Wooldridge. Random House, 1996.

Wild Mind: Living the Writer's Life, Natalie Goldberg. Bantam Books, 1990.

Writing Down the Bones: Freeing the Writer Within, Natalie Goldberg. Shambhala Publications, 1986.

Grammar and other ugly topics

The Chicago Manual of Style, 15th ed. University of Chicago Press, 2003.

Elements of Style, William Strunk Jr. and E.B. White. Macmillan, 1979.

Sleeping Dogs Don't Lay: Practical Advice for the Grammatically Challenged; Richard Lederer and Richard Dowis; St. Martins Griffin; 1999.

The Synonym Finder, J.I. Rodale, Nancy LaRoche, Laurence Urdang. Warner Books; 1986.

Woe is I: The Grammarphobe's Guide to Better English, Patricia O'Conner. Riverhead Books, 1998.

Words Fail Me: What Everyone Who Writes Should Know About Writing, Patricia O'Conner. Harcourt Brace, 1999.

Marketing and Publication

Formatting & Submitting Your Manuscript, 2nd ed., Cynthia Laufenberg. Writer's Digest Books, 2004.

The First Five Pages: A Writer's Guide to Staying Out of the Rejection Pile, Noah Lukeman. Fireside Books (Simon and Schuster), 2002.

Writer's Market, Writer's Digest Books, Annual Publication.

Other Resources

"The Short Short" Vera Henry, from *The Writer's Digest Handbook of Short Story Writing*, vol. 2. Writer's Digest Books, 1988.

Appendix C

Online Resources

Flash Fiction

What is Flash Fiction? by Kezia Richmond

http://www.bloc-online.com/aboutwriting/articles/
flash_fiction.htm

Flashes On The Meridian: Dazzled by Flash Fiction
by Pamelyn Casto

http://www.heelstone.com/meridian/meansarticle1.html

Writing Flash Fiction by G. W. Thomas

http://www.fictionfactor.com/guests/flashfiction.html

Flashing Your Setting by S. Joan Popek

Good article on including setting in your flash fiction.

http://www.sjoanpopek.com/writeflash.html

Fiction in a Flash

This site is a great resource for flash fiction, providing
articles and links to markets, as well as access to a flash
fiction newsgroup.

http://www.fictioninaflash.com

Urban Legends

Urban Legends and Folklore on About.com

"The starting place for exploring Urban Legends and Folklore on the Web: Internet hoaxes, rumors, urban legends and urban myths debunked. "

http://urbanlegends.about.com/

Scambusters: Don't Believe Everything You Read

http://www.scambusters.org/legends.html

How Urban Legends Work by Tom Harris

Detailed explanation of how urban legends come about and how they become widely believed. Very interesting article.

http://www.howstuffworks.com/urban-legend.htm

Myths, Fables

Myths and Legends

If you are looking for information on the myths or legends of any world culture, this is the place to start. This site contains Web links, suggested print titles, story collections of myths from around the world, academic studies of myth, mythical creatures, and a whole lot more.

http://members.bellatlantic.net/~vze33gpz/myth.html

Appendix D

Contributor Notes

Bruce Boston is the author of forty books and chapbooks, including the novel *Stained Glass Rain* and the best-of-fiction collection *Masque of Dreams*. His stories and poems have appeared in hundreds of publications, including the *Nebula Awards Showcase* and *Year's Best Fantasy and Horror*, and received numerous awards, most notably the Pushcart Prize, the Asimov's Readers' Award, and the Grand Master Award of the Science Fiction Poetry Association. For more information, visit his website at http://hometown.aol.com/bruboston.

Angie DeRosa is an award-winning business reporter for *Plastics News*, a weekly trade journal owned by Crain Communications, Inc. In 1999, she graduated with honors from Kent State University in Kent, Ohio, with a bachelor's degree in journalism and mass communication. She lives in Columbus, Ohio, with her husband and two Balinese cats. Of the stories she's written, "How To Treat a Man" is among her favorites.

Phoebe Kate Foster is an associate editor at *Pop Matters*, an online magazine of global culture, and assistant editor at *The Dead Mule*, a Southern literary ezine. Her short fiction has been nominated for the Pushcart Prize and included in several anthologies, and has appeared/is forthcoming in *Prairie Schooner*, *Eclectica*, *Vestal Review*, *Paumanok Review*, *flashquake*, *Carve*, *Wilmington Blues*, *Word Riot*, *Fiction Warehouse*, *Slow Trains*, *Spillway Review* and *Electric Acorn* (Ireland), among others.

Cathie B. Hamilton is a thirty-something mother of two young sons. She lives with her husband, children, and a menagerie of animals in Frederick, Maryland where she practices as a speech-language pathologist. She cannot imagine letting a day go by without reading or writing, and her work has been published in *flashquake* and *Frederick's Child Magazine*.

Melissa Hess, an award-winning professional writer and graphic artist, is currently working as a technical writer in the telecom software industry, developing manuals and online help systems. She holds a graduate degree in Scientific and Technical Communication from Bowling Green State University and an undergraduate degree in Speech Communication from Miami University. Melissa lives in the Columbus, Ohio, area with her husband and two children. She can be contacted by e-mail at mhess2@columbus.rr.com.

M.K. Hobson lives in Oregon with her husband, her daughter, and a bright blue fish. Her fiction has appeared online (*SCIFICTION*, *Vestal Review*, *flashquake*) and in print (*Magazine of Fantasy and Science Fiction*, *Talus* and *Scree*). More of her work can be viewed at her Web site, www.demimonde.com.

Beverly Jackson is a poet and writer widely published in print on the Internet. Her work can be found in *Rattle*, *Melic Review*, *Zoetrope All Story Extra*, *Vestal Review*, *In Posse Review*, to name a few. She is also runs a small press, Lit Pot Press, which publishes poetry, literary fiction, and a quarterly print journal, *INK POT*, and has an active online e-zine, LitPot.com. You can reach her at litpot@veryfast.biz.

Derrick Lin lives a quiet happy life in San Mateo, California. He has studied at Stanford University's Writer Workshops. He has previously been published in *flashquake*.

Clint Meadows is a 22-year-old year bagboy whose works have appeared in *42opus*, *flashquake*, and various school-related literary journals. His twin brother, Dustin, is an aspiring ninja. Clint can reached at Clint129@yahoo.com.

Lori Ruediger, a senior technical editor in the telecom software industry, spent more than 20 years in higher education, writing and editing academic publications and also teaching both writing and editing. An Oregonian who has lived in Chile, Afghanistan, and assorted U.S. states, she now happily calls New Hampshire home.

Marge Ballif Simon teaches art in Florida and freelances as a writer-poet-illustrator for genre and mainstream publications such as *Nebula Awards 32*, *Strange Horizons*, *flashquake*, *The Urbanite*, *Tomorrow Magazine of Speculative Fiction* (www.tomororrow.com), and many others. She has been published in the anthologies, *High Fantastic*, and *Nebula Anthology 32*. She edits the *Star*Line* (digest of the SFPA). Her poetry collections include *Eonian Variations*, *Night Smoke*, and *Artist of Antithesis*. Web site: http://hometown.aol.com/margsimon

Charles Tuomi lives in southeastern Massachusetts. He is a software engineer and speculative fiction writer. His short fiction has appeared online in *Chiaroscuro*, *Ideomancer*, and *flashquake*. His Web site is at: http://www.geocities.com/c_tuomi.

About the Author

Michael Wilson has been teaching creative writing classes and facilitating writer's groups for over 7 years and was an award-winning Contributing Editor for The Writer's Block at Suite101.com. He has a BA (with Honors) in English from Ohio University, and has been a featured guest speaker at the Thurber House, the Maumee Valley Writer's Conference and the Columbus Writer's Conference. He is also the publisher and editor of *Grist for the Muse* a monthly creative writing e-newsletter. *Flash Writing: How to Write, Revise and Publish Stories Under 1000 Words Long* is his first book.

Please feel free to e-mail Michael with questions or comments about *Flash Writing* at michael@wilson.us

Grist for the Muse

Is your **FREE** monthly creative writing e-newsletter designed to get you writing and keep you writing. With writing exercises, advice, book and website reviews, and occasional shameless self-promotion, *Grist for the Muse* helps you maximize your writing potential. To sign up:

- Go to the web at this URL: http://www.topica.com/lists/Grist_for_the_Muse

- Or via email by sending a BLANK email to: Grist_for_the_Muse-subscribe@topica.com

PASS THE FLASH ALONG!

Order additional copies of *Flash Writing: How to Write, Revise and Publish Stories of 1,000 Words or Less* for $14.95 each for each of the writers in your life!

Please send a check or money order for $17.95 ($14.95 plus $3.00 shipping and handling) Ohio residents please add 6.75% sales tax ($1.01).

Name _____

Mailing Address _____

_____

City _____

State and Zip Code _____

E-mail address
(optional) _____

Please make your check or money order payable to and return to:

Michael Wilson
200 Rainbow Drive NE
Lancaster, Ohio 43130-8846

You can also order the book online direct from the Virtual Bookworm bookstore using your Visa or Mastercard at:

http://www.virtualbookworm.com/merchant.mvc?LNG=en-US&Screen=PLST

Or contact me via e-mail at michael@wilson.us for PayPal purchasing information.

Breinigsville, PA USA
07 July 2010
241353BV00003B/11/A